FIRST PETER

The Deeper Life Pulpit Commentary

FIRST PETER

Strategic Imperatives for Suffering Saints

ARNOLD R. FLEAGLE

Christian Publications
CAMP HILL, PENNSYLVANIA

Christian Publications, Inc.
3825 Hartzdale Drive, Camp Hill, PA 17011

Faithful, biblical publishing since 1883

ISBN: 0-87509-625-5
LOC Catalog Card Number: 97-65426

© 1997 by Christian Publications, Inc.

CONTENTS

ACKNOWLEDGMENTS

This commentary on First Peter has been a team endeavor. Dr. Neill Foster, one of my mentors, invited me to participate in this significant project. Immanuel Alliance Church of Mechanicsburg, Pennsylvania, and Stow Alliance Fellowship of Stow, Ohio, provided ample opportunity to write and "lab test" its contents. My executive secretaries, Jeannie Brenneman and Ann Madeira, exercised their many personal and clerical gifts to accelerate completion of the task. Dr. Elio Cuccaro invested time with me which contributed to the project's substance and style. David Fessenden, Tomi Duttry, Lisa Rohrick and Janet Hixon have "sandpapered" the manuscript I presented them. My "lady," Faye, has brought me many second winds throughout this journey. Finally, one of my main motivations for writing revolves around my two sons, Matthew and Marc. My noble hope is that they will embrace the Christian imperatives folded into Peter's transforming letter.

1

Peter's Introduction

1 Peter 1:1-2

Peter, an apostle of Jesus Christ,
To God's elect, strangers in the world, scattered throughout Pontus, Galatia, Cappadocia, Asia and Bithynia, who have been chosen according to the foreknowledge of God the Father, through the sanctifying work of the Spirit, for obedience to Jesus Christ and sprinkling by his blood:
Grace and peace be yours in abundance. (1 Peter 1:1-2)

ONE LETTER CONTAINS THE CLOUT to alter the direction of a person's entire life. *One letter* can birth a student's academic career at a prestigious university or abort it. *One letter* can propel an author to submit his manuscript for publication or it can crush that author's spirit to the degree he will never try to write

again. *One letter* can chronicle a mother's successful bout with cancer or condemn that special lady
to a short lease on life.

Every letter does not bear such capacity; many
are superficial and trite. Yet everyone has opened
a letter which has functioned like a brisk October
wind striking a single leaf as it rests upon the
autumn ground. There is movement, a change of
direction and a new destiny. Peter's first letter is a
document designed to influence, instruct and inspire these "leaves from God's tree."

First Peter is a member of the group of New Testament letters labeled the "catholic" or "general epistles." These letters lack the indication of being
written to a single locality, in contrast to the Pauline
letters written to specific cities, regions or persons.
They are titled according to their traditional
authors, as is the practice in the four Gospels.

First Peter has many enthusiastic advocates
who praise its useability, relevance and popularity.
William Barclay, the renowned Scottish New
Testament scholar, wrote that "of all the General
Epistles it is probably true that First Peter is the
best known and loved, and the most read."[1] Everett F. Harrison in his *Introduction to the New Testament* stated that "among the so-called Catholic
Epistles none has been more widely used or more
highly respected during the history of the church
than this one attributed to Simon Peter."[2] E.J.
Goodspeed characterized this charming letter
with this assessment: "First Peter is one of the
most moving pieces of persecution literature."[3]

Edwin A. Blum in *The Expositor's Bible Commentary* described the flavor of First Peter in these terms: "The tone of First Peter is a warm pastoral one, full of encouragement."[4]

These glowing recommendations provide more than adequate rationale to be enthused about this small but significant letter. But beyond these plaudits there is the content of this epistle which offers the contemporary Christian a "boot camp" on how to survive in the hostile environment of a post-Christian culture. Peter's manuscript is directed to scattered strangers (1:1) who were staring persecution in the face. They constituted a demographic minority and desperately looked forward to the second coming of Jesus Christ. First Peter is an instructional manual on the nonnegotiables of the Christian lifestyle, a recital of the imperatives of the faith which enable believers to be resilient despite the afflictions which embrace their lives. The word *imperative* comes from the Latin word *imperativus*, "to command." The word *imperator* was attached to the Roman emperor or the Roman military commander. When the imperator gave the imperative there were no options, no alternatives, no excuses. The citizen, soldier or servant in those days of the Roman Empire obeyed! Peter has woven throughout this letter imperatives which are the expectation for the Christian in spite of his environment, opposition or cost.

Make no mistake about the prevailing winds that blew against those first century adherents of Christianity. Peter employs the word *suffer* a dozen times in this brief letter. He overtly announces his purpose for writing this document near the end of his communique: "I have written to you briefly, encouraging you and testifying that this is the true grace of God. *Stand fast in it*" (5:12, emphasis mine).

The anemic and fainthearted faith of believers, which is too often manifest in our society, is a cause for frustration and despair. A.W. Tozer wrote:

> The contemporary moral climate does not favor a faith as tough and fibrous as that taught by our Lord and His apostles. The delicate, brittle saints being produced in our religious hothouses today are hardly to be compared with the committed, expendable believers who once gave their witness among men.[5]

Peter is addressing followers of Jesus Christ who have their "feet to the fire." He is cheering them on and challenging them with passionate exhortations expressed through the conduit of his pen. He is a qualified advisor because of the persecutions which plagued him during Jesus' ministry and the apostolic period. Peter's name is derived from the Greek word *petros*, which means *rock* (cf. Matthew 16:18), and his purpose was to stabilize and harden these believers into "living stones" (see 1 Peter 2:5) that could withstand the trials and tests of fire and rain.

The Writer (1:1a)

Peter is one of the most fascinating men of the New Testament era. A fisherman by trade, he was brought to Jesus by his brother, Andrew (John 1:42). He responded to the invitation "follow me" (Matthew 4:19) and became one of the most influential Christians in the first century.

Peter was one-third of the inner circle of the disciples. He, along with John and James, was privileged to witness events that the other nine disciples did not experience. Only these three men were invited to go into Jairus' house and observe the raising of his dead daughter (Luke 8:51). Only these three men went with Jesus up on a mountain to pray, and it was at this venue that the transfiguration occurred (9:28-36). It was this trio which Jesus kept nearest to Him in the Garden of Gethsemane in His agonizing moments of prayer before He was apprehended by the soldiers (Matthew 26:37).

His legacy in the faith is anything but consistent. His failures are well documented. He walked on water but then became fearful and began to sink (14:29-30). After Jesus made His prediction that He would die and be raised from the dead, Peter had the audacity to rebuke Him (16:22). And his most infamous failure was his triple denial of Jesus Christ when he was questioned about his association with Him (26:69-75).

Nevertheless, Peter became one of the greatest heroes of the early Church, second only to Paul.

Heaven had cast him into a special role. It was Peter who spoke the great confession, "You are the Christ, the Son of the living God" (16:16). He was the first disciple to go into the tomb after Jesus' resurrection (John 20:6). He was a leader in the group which awaited the filling of the Holy Spirit at Pentecost (Acts 1:15). In the post-Pentecost days of the early Church Peter is recognized as a powerful preacher and fearless witness to the gospel of Jesus Christ. He suffered the same fate as his Lord, being crucified in Rome. Legend chronicles that Peter requested to be crucified upside down because he was not worthy to die in the same manner as his Messiah.[6]

Peter designates himself in the first statement of this letter as an apostle of Jesus Christ. The word literally means "one that is sent from." Peter was a carrier, a messenger, an ambassador, dispersing the good news of his Lord. His postal route would encompass Jerusalem, Palestine, Syria and finally the capital of the Roman Empire.

The Recipients (1:1b)

This letter was targeted to the Roman provinces that covered a major part of Asia Minor (modern Turkey). Since the author does not employ the Aramaic name Cephas (John 1:42), but rather uses the Greek name Peter, he is intentionally being sensitive to Gentiles in his audience. However, Christian Jews were numbered among the groups in the regions mentioned, though they were in the minority.

"To God's elect" (1 Peter 1:1) indicates that the readers were believers. Election is a strategic doctrine in understanding the grace of God which has been directed to all those who have been redeemed. To be elected means "to be picked or chosen from among others." According to Ephesians 1:4, this election was made prior to the creation of our world: "For he chose us in him before the creation of the world to be holy and blameless in his sight." John Calvin pointed out that the timing of the selection preempted any merit on the part of humanity when he wrote, "the very time of election shows it to be free; for what could we have deserved, or in what did our merit consist, before the world was made?"[7] The word for church is *ekklesia*, "the called out ones," and pertains to those who have been separated from the world for a life of obedience and service to God. The Church is to be a counterculture, a theme that Peter would refer to later in his manuscript. Jesus also incorporated the concept of the elect into His discourse about the end times in Matthew 24. The *elect* are those who are gathered by the angels when the loud trumpet call of God is sounded (Matthew 24:31).

This select group is also a scattered band of believers who find themselves outside the "comfort zone" of life. They do not have the "home field advantage." A.T. Robertson, in his *Word Pictures in the New Testament*, describes them in these terms: "The picture in the metaphor here is that heaven is our native country and we are only temporary sojourners here on earth. . . . The Christian is a

pilgrim on his way to the homeland."[8] The journey of those first-century disciples was indeed a
"pilgrim's progress."

The Process of Election (1:2a-b)

Foreknowledge is a component of the selection
process. The *choice* of the elect is predicated upon
God's panoramic view of human history. God's
prevenient grasp of all that will transpire permits
Him to precisely know who should be the elect.
Foreknowledge is not equivalent to foreordination
or predestination; however, the two often work in
tandem in God's plan for the world. Paul weaves
both into his Roman treatise, "For those God
foreknew he also predestined to be conformed to
the likeness of his Son, that he might be the first-
born among many brothers" (8:29). This theology
of foreknowing, if embraced by these scattered
and suffering adherents of the Christian faith, provides significant solace because the victims are
aware that God foresaw their dilemma before it
afflicted them. Therefore, Paul would encourage
them to remember "that in all things God works
for the good of those who love him, who have
been called according to his purpose" (8:28).

The elect are sanctified by the Holy Spirit. To
sanctify means "to set apart for a special work or
service." The Spirit is the person of the Trinity
who administers this consecration. Again, the "select team" nature of the Church of Jesus Christ is
highlighted. The Holy Spirit is not only the
"travel Agent," He is the "change Agent."

The Purpose of Election (1:2c)

Obedience is a nonnegotiable for the elect. The Great Commission which Jesus left His Church explicitly details the *imperative of obedience:* "Therefore go and make disciples of all nations, baptizing them in the name of the Father and of the Son and of the Holy Spirit, and teaching them to *obey* everything I have commanded you. And surely I am with you always, to the very end of the age" (Matthew 28:19-20, emphasis added). The Christian must possess more than orthodoxy (right doctrine); the Christian must manifest orthopraxis (right living). In the opening of his Roman letter, Paul linked obedience and faith to communicate the rationale for calling people out from sin and bondage: "Through him and for his name's sake, we received grace and apostleship to call people from among all the Gentiles to the obedience that comes from faith" (Romans 1:5). Jesus Christ inseparably linked love and obedience and made compliance with His commands the litmus test for authentic discipleship. He hammered away at this theme in John 14:15, 23 and 24. Perhaps John 14:15 is the most direct statement: "If you love me, you will obey what I command." Obedience may be the MVT (Most Valuable Term) in the entire New Testament because it connects with so many crucial concepts, such as love, faith, hope and suffering.

Peter is aware of his readers' pain, and he reminds them at the outset of this letter that their election is to result in compliance and obedience. The imperative of obedience often requires sacrifice. In the book of Acts, Peter and the other apostles demonstrated their commitment to obey even when their lives were in jeopardy. When called before the Sanhedrin they boldly declared: "We must obey God rather than men!" (Acts 5:29). This obedience was displayed during the Reformation era when Martin Luther appeared before the Diet of Worms. The inquisitor asked him to repudiate his beliefs, and his response still rings loudly today:

> Unless I am convicted by Scripture and plain reason—I do not accept the authority of popes and councils, for they have contradicted each other—my conscience is captive to the Word of God. I cannot and I will not recant anything, for to go against conscience is neither right nor safe. Here I stand, I cannot do otherwise. God help me. Amen.[9]

The Bible has many examples of men and women who did not hold fast to their convictions and principles, who waffled when God's Word had been clearly enunciated. King Saul was instructed to exterminate the Amalekites and their oxen, sheep, donkeys and camels. When Samuel's ears registered the bleating of sheep echoing off the slopes of Mt. Carmel, he probed Israel's king and discovered the evidence of disobedience. Saul rationalized that his army "spared the best of the sheep and cattle to sacrifice to the LORD your God" (1 Samuel 15:15). The judge's gavel was swift and terminal:

But Samuel replied:

"Does the LORD delight in burnt offerings
    and sacrifices
  as much as in obeying the voice of the
    LORD?
To obey is better than sacrifice,
  and to heed is better than the fat of rams.
For rebellion is like the sin of divination,
  and arrogance like the evil of idolatry.
Because you have rejected the word of the
    LORD,
  he has rejected you as king."
    (15:22-23)

Obedience is nonnegotiable even for mighty monarchs. Those selected by God are to be meticulous in their adherence to His will and Word. The elect of Peter's first-century audience and the elect of our contemporary crowd are no different regarding this expectation. The Christian race is a marathon and not a sprint. Obedience must be as frequent as the temptation to defect and detour from the narrow path that God has mapped out for His children. Nietzsche, of all people, packaged this perseverance of obedience when he wrote: "The essential thing in 'heaven and earth' is . . . that there should be a long obedience in the

same direction; that thereby results, and has always resulted, in the long run, something which
has made life worth living."[10]

Peter also incorporates the atonement into his
greeting. "Sprinkling by his blood" (1:2) is a direct
reference to the sacrificial death of Jesus Christ for
the sins of His people. Exodus 24:6-8 includes a
graphic description of Moses sprinkling blood on
the altar and on the people, the first action sym-
bolizing God's forgiveness and the second action
commemorating the oath of obedience that the
people made in response to the disclosure of the
Lord's words and laws. These covenantal acts are
embryonic and serve as commentary on the new
covenant which is executed by Jesus Christ on the
cross. Hebrews 9:11-14 summarizes the sprinkling
which is appropriated to the believer:

> When Christ came as high priest of the
> good things that are already here, he went
> through the greater and more perfect taber-
> nacle that is not man-made, that is to say,
> not a part of this creation. He did not enter
> by means of the blood of goats and calves;
> but he entered the Most Holy Place once for
> all by his own blood, having obtained eter-
> nal redemption. The blood of goats and
> bulls and the ashes of a heifer sprinkled on
> those who are ceremonially unclean sanctify
> them so that they are outwardly clean. How
> much more, then, will the blood of Christ,
> who through the eternal Spirit offered him-

self unblemished to God, cleanse our consciences from acts that lead to death, so that we may serve the living God!

"Grace and peace" are often paired in first-century letters, both sacred and secular, but Peter's employment of them is qualified by the word *abundance.* There is an overflow of God's unmerited favor *(charis)* and a surplus of God's reconciling power *(eirene)* which the apostle aspires to be actualized in the life of these weary strangers in an unfriendly and inhospitable land.

What follows this introduction (1:1-2) is a recital of the imperatives which are core values of the authentic Christian. These imperatives, if followed, will result in "making the invisible Christ visible" before a world that so desperately needs to see Him. Peter wanted the theology of those believers to become biography. May those who study this letter find that reality to be true in their own Christian lives.

Discussion Questions for Further Study

1. What is our society's response to imperatives or commands? Do you think this affects how people respond to God's Word (such as the imperatives in First Peter)?

2. What are Peter's qualifications to write about life and ministry?

3. What are your thoughts on this statement:

"Obedience may be the most valuable word in the New Testament"?

4. Why is the "blood of Jesus Christ" still an appropriate issue in contemporary culture? Why do some people find it objectionable?

Endnotes

[1] William Barclay, *The Letters of James and Peter, The Daily Study Bible Series*, Vol. 14 (Philadelphia: Westminster Press, 1976), 138.

[2] Everett F. Harrison, *Introduction to the New Testament* (Grand Rapids, MI: Eerdmans, 1964), 394.

[3] E.J. Goodspeed, quoted in Barclay, *The Letters of James and Peter*, 138.

[4] Leon Morris et. al., *Hebrews-Revelation, The Expositor's Bible Commentary*, Vol. 12, ed. Frank E. Gaebelein (Grand Rapids, MI: Zondervan, 1981), 213.

[5] A.W. Tozer, *Renewed Day by Day, Vol. 1* (Camp Hill, PA: Christian Publications, 1980), September 4.

[6] Eusebius, *Ecclesiastical History*.

[7] David W. Torrance and Thomas F. Torrance, eds., *Calvin's Commentaries, The Epistles of Paul the Apostle to the Galatians, Ephesians, Philippians and Colossians*, Vol. 3, trans. T.H.L. Parker (Grand Rapids, MI: Eerdmans, 1974), 125.

[8] Archibald Thomas Robertson, *Word Pictures in the New Testament, The General Epistles and The Revelation of John*, Vol. 6 (Grand Rapids, MI: Baker, 1933), 79.

[9] Martin Luther, cited in Tim Dowley, ed., *Eerdman's Handbook of the History of Christianity* (Grand Rapids, MI: Eerdmans, 1977), 364.

[10] Friedrich Nietzsche, *Beyond God and Evil*, trans. Helen Zimmern (London: 1907), Section 188, 106-109.

2

The Imperative to Stand in Faith

1 Peter 1:3-12

Praise be to the God and Father of our Lord Jesus Christ! In his great mercy he has given us new birth into a living hope through the resurrection of Jesus Christ from the dead, and into an inheritance that can never perish, spoil or fade—kept in heaven for you, who through faith are shielded by God's power until the coming of the salvation that is ready to be revealed in the last time. In this you greatly rejoice, though now for a little while you may have had to suffer grief in all kinds of trials. These have come so that your faith—of greater worth than gold, which perishes even though refined by fire—may be proved genuine and may result in praise, glory and honor when Jesus Christ is revealed. Though you have not seen him, you love him; and even though you do not see him now, you believe in him and are filled with an inexpressible and glo-

*rious joy, for you are receiving the goal of your
faith, the salvation of your souls.*

*Concerning this salvation, the prophets, who
spoke of the grace that was to come to you,
searched intently and with the greatest care, trying to find out the time and circumstances to
which the Spirit of Christ in them was pointing
when he predicted the sufferings of Christ and
the glories that would follow. It was revealed to
them that they were not serving themselves but
you, when they spoke of the things that have now
been told you by those who have preached the
gospel to you by the Holy Spirit sent from
heaven. Even angels long to look into these
things. (1 Peter 1:3-12)*

"**D**IFFICULTIES ARE THE DIVINE IN-
CENTIVES which demand and develop our confidence in the divine
faithfulness and love," wrote A.B. Simpson.[1] Peter's perspective on suffering has this same positive flavor. Although he had been persecuted and
was writing to fellow believers who had tasted of
"suffering's stew," Peter took the position that
God was using suffering to accomplish His plans
for the planet and in particular for His people.
The apostle follows the greeting of First Peter 1:1-
2 with a significant amount of text devoted to this
principle: *Stand fast in your faith*. This is a divine
imperative, to "take the lemon and make lemon-
ade."

Peter opens this section on suffering with a doxology: "Praise be to the God and Father of our Lord Jesus Christ!" The Greek word for *praise* is *eulogetos*, made up of *eu* (good) and *logeo* (to speak). The English word *eulogy*, the "good word" spoken about a deceased person, is derived from *eulogetos*. The apostle had a good word for His God. William Barclay elaborates on the difference this doxology manifests from a traditional Jewish doxology. He writes:

> For a Jew the commonest of all beginnings to prayer was, "Blessed art thou, O God." The Christian takes over that prayer with a difference. His prayer begins, "Blessed be the God and Father of our Lord Jesus Christ." He is not praying to a distant, unknown God; he is praying to the God who is like Jesus and to whom, through Jesus Christ, he may come with childlike confidence.[2]

The Christian is to be like a nightingale, filling the night season with the songs of celebration and praise. Peter has not put his praise on the shelf; therefore, his environment and this epistle resonates with joyful song!

Renewed in Mercy (1:3-5)

Someone has remarked, "A Christian's pay isn't that great, but the benefits are out of this world." In reality, the Christian is never paid because the heavenly Father has graciously poured out upon us His lavish mercy, an endowment which is not based upon our achievements. As Peter begins his recital of God's "benefit package," he prefaces the particulars with this phrase, "in his great mercy."[3] Mercy is a term of sympathy, but sympathy coupled with actions. It is not a sterile "sympathy," but a Good Samaritan sympathy that does not walk by the need with just an emotional acknowledgment. God is the ultimate Good Samaritan. He is the God Who Acts, not just the God Who Looks. Those who hold to deism believe that God started the "clock of history" and then backed away and did not interfere. The Bible does not endorse such a laissez-faire philosophy.

When Moses encountered God at the burning bush, the Scriptures say that God not only looked at Israel's dilemma, but actively involved Himself in its resolution:

> The LORD said, "I have indeed seen the misery of my people in Egypt. I have heard them crying out because of their slave drivers, and I am concerned about their suffering. So I have come down to rescue them from the hand of the Egyptians and to bring them up out of that land into a good and spacious land, a land flowing with milk and honey—the home of the Canaanites, Hittites, Amorites, Perizzites, Hivites and Jebusites." (Exodus 3:7-8)

It should be noted that this deliverance did not come for four centuries. However, God's delays are not God's denials. He has a timetable, and in His time He makes everything beautiful (Ecclesiastes 3:11). This was mandatory theology for those first-century believers who did not always witness an immediate response to their afflictions, but God is rich in mercy and He does act to counter the effects of our sins and the sins of others. A.W. Tozer defined mercy as "an attribute of God, an infinite and inexhaustible energy within the divine nature which disposes God to be *actively compassionate*" (emphasis added).[4] Our God's response to our unholy rebellion and resistance has been mercy. A hymn writer captured it well:

> When all Thy mercies, O my God,
>   My rising soul surveys,
> Transported with the view, I'm lost
>   In wonder, love, and praise.[5]

The New Birth

This great mercy translates into many "line items" of blessing. The first benefit of mercy Peter cites is the "new birth" (1 Peter 1:3). The merciful Father has presented us a clean slate, a second chance, a fresh new page upon which to write the exploits of our life. Jesus had a rather extended discussion with Nicodemus on this subject and delineated the necessity of the new birth for those that desired to enter the kingdom of heaven. John 3:3-8 is the defining passage on this subject:

> In reply Jesus declared, "I tell you the truth, no one can see the kingdom of God unless he is born again."
>
> "How can a man be born when he is old?" Nicodemus asked. "Surely he cannot enter a second time into his mother's womb to be born!"
>
> Jesus answered, "I tell you the truth, no one can enter the kingdom of God unless he is born of water and the Spirit. Flesh gives birth to flesh, but the Spirit gives birth to spirit. You should not be surprised at my saying, 'You must be born again.' The wind blows wherever it pleases. You hear its sound, but you cannot tell where it comes from or where it is going. So it is with everyone born of the Spirit."

The new birth was not an option, and so the mercy of God provided this indispensable ingredient for the Christian's portfolio.

The Living Hope

A second benefit of mercy is the "living hope" (1:3). Both the adjective *living* and the noun *hope* are favorite terms Peter employs in his first letter. A.T. Robertson observes that "Peter is fond of the word 'living.' "[6] In these verses *living* is descriptive of God's Word, Jesus Christ as "the living Stone" and believers as "living stones." Peter's hope has a strong pulse, which can be traced to the heartbeat of the gospel, to the life, death and resurrection of Jesus Christ. *Hope* is another of Peter's favorite terms, and he weaves it into the manuscript in five different places. Besides the "living hope," this vital concept for persecuted disciples is found in the following verses (emphasis added in each):

> Therefore, prepare your minds for action; be self-controlled; set your *hope* fully on the grace to be given you when Jesus Christ is revealed. (1:13)

> Through him you believe in God, who raised him from the dead and glorified him, and so your faith and *hope* are in God. (1:21)

> For this is the way the holy women of the past who put their *hope* in God used to make themselves beautiful. They were submissive to their own husbands. (3:5)

> But in your hearts set apart Christ as Lord. Always be prepared to give an answer to everyone who asks you to give the reason for the *hope* that you have. But do this with gentleness and respect. (3:15)

First Peter has been nicknamed "the letter of hope," and A.B. Simpson compared its author with two other Christian notables with this assessment:

"Peter is indeed the apostle of hope, as Paul is the apostle of faith, and John the messenger of love."[7]

The Inheritance

A third benefit is the "inheritance" (1:4) which is being held in escrow in heaven until the believer comes to possess it! Our culture produces many successful people who will dispose of tremendous resources when they die. However, sometimes the heirs discover that tax laws, new inventions or a decline in property values have eroded the expectations and real value of the estate. But the inheritance of God's child will not perish, spoil or fade, for it is being kept in heaven, and heaven has an indestructible safe-deposit box.

Warren Wiersbe made this meaningful affirmation: "We are included in Christ's last will and testament, and we share the glory with Him."[8] Many heirs have counted on a full cupboard of "goodies" being passed on to them following the death of a loved one and then were disappointed because the cupboard was bare. The inheritance of the pilgrim who hopes in Christ is beyond comprehension and decay.

First Peter 1:5 enters into this discussion on inheritance and the heirs who are designated to receive it with a balance that is necessary to guarantee the long-term preservation of the estate. "Through faith," which describes the function or activity of the believer in this preservation process, is balanced by "are shielded by God's power." There is a human or horizontal action of faith which works in *tandem* with the divine or vertical action of shielding. Peter points out this stabilizing partnership between the sovereign God and the believer who exercises limited sovereignty by asserting his or her confidence in the Protector during times of tribulation. The disciples of Jesus Christ are not to be passive puppets, but active soldiers progressing toward the day when the priceless inheritance is awarded and the struggle made worthwhile.

This divine-human partnership results in the consummation of the salvation which God intended and the persecuted have so sacrificially pursued. The term *salvation* is used three times at the front of this letter (1:5, 9-10 and 2:2). It does not occur any other place in this communication. This beneficial synopsis illuminates Peter's use of the term:

> In I Peter the apostle uses *soteria*, along with a number of expressions, to express final salvation. Christians are guarded by God's power through faith for this salvation, which is already there, but which will be revealed only in the last time (1:5). Christians "grow up" to this salvation through the spiritual food which they receive through preaching and teaching (2:2), so that finally they reach the goal of their faith . . . the glorification which is to be theirs (1:9). Already the prophets had pondered on and prophesied about it (1:10).[9]

Similar to the dynamic concept of the *kingdom*, which is a "now but not yet" doctrine, salvation incorporates *three tenses:* the past, the present and the future. The pilgrim must remember that salvation began at conversion, is occurring during the days and nights which follow it and will be consummated in the future. Salvation is an elastic concept which enables the believer to bend but not break as he or she faces the trials of the present earthly existence. The Christian's edge lies in the fact that the final chapter of human history reveals that Jesus wins, and this "foreknowledge" sustains him or her when the ball is fumbled or when poor officiating by this world's referees rule against the team and the player.

Refined by Fire (1:6-7)

In anticipation of their future deliverance, God's people can rejoice despite Peter's recognition that "for a little while" they may have "to suffer grief in all kinds of trials" (1:6). We must be aware that our symbol is not a pillow but a cross. However, the cross becomes a plus sign when we realize that God is working through our brokenness to accomplish blessing! The *imperative to rejoice in suffering* was a trademark of many who pledged allegiance to Jesus Christ in the first century. Acts 5:41 records this scenario following the disciples' flogging by their Jewish opponents: "The apostles left the Sanhedrin, rejoicing because they had been counted *worthy* of suffering disgrace for the Name" (emphasis added).

Paul advocates a joyful attitude in suffering in his letter to the Romans: "Not only so, but we also rejoice in our sufferings, because we know that suffering produces perseverance; perseverance, character; and character, hope" (5:3-4). And James' letter, sometimes labeled "the New Testament Ecclesiastes," advises us that we should practice a "suffering math" that counts in this manner: "My brethren, count it all joy when ye fall into divers temptations; knowing this, that the trying of your faith worketh patience" (1:2-3, KJV). The saint is to view these sufferings as short in duration, "little while" griefs which come in "all kinds of trials." The authentic believer will take the panoramic view of history. E. Stanley Jones, Methodist missionary to India, wrote: "Christians, above all others, are people of the long view, the long purpose, and the long plan."[10] Spiritual shortsightedness leads to defection and defeat. The dynamic Christian views the bump as a step on the way to the summit! As the believer encounters troubles, these negatives provide a lab for new understandings of God, the Christian faith and an enlarged self-understanding. The trials become trails!

What is the grand purpose of the trials? They have come to prove the genuineness of an individual's faith (1:7). The word for proving or trying the faith is *dokimazo* which sheds increased light on this subject of suffering. One commentator states that:

It literally means "to put someone to the test with the expectation of showing that he is worthy of being approved." It was used in the New Testament days to describe the final examination all medical students passed before they were given the right to set up their own practice.[11]

The suffering exams enable us to graduate to God's glorious commencement ceremony!

Billy Graham recorded this staccato-like observation in his book, *World Aflame:* "Fire purifies or destroys."[12] The refiner's fire is a redemptive factor in the reproduction of Jesus Christ in His people! The uncomfortable heat of the refiner's fire will blow out from the furnaces of the world, the flesh and the devil. The byproducts, however, are a faith with integrity and a person of Christian mettle, of value which exceeds the preciousness of gold (1:7). There are no exceptions to "the refiner's fire."

The ancient cultures valued gold, and as we approach the twenty-first century, gold still has a prominent place in the hierarchy of valuables. Consider this helpful commentary on the analogy:

Gold is one of man's most prized objects. When it is refined, its impurities are removed by a fiery process. Though extremely durable, gold belongs to the perishing world order. Faith, which is more valuable than gold because it lasts longer and reaches beyond the temporal order, is purified in the tests of life. Gold, not faith, is presently valued by men. But God will set his stamp of approval on faith that has been tested and shows this when Christ is revealed. Then the believer will openly share in the praise, glory, and honor of God.[13]

Peter prescribes the formula for faith's gold, the refiner's fire. When you are tested by fire you must remember that as the flames dance about you, *you* have the opportunity to experience the triumph of faith!

Reinforced by Love, Belief and Joy (1:8-9)

What is *vision*? George Barna defines vision in these terms: "Vision . . . is a clear mental image of a preferable future imparted by God to His chosen servants and is based upon an accurate understanding of God, self and circumstances."[14] Vision looks beyond the existing state and envisions a new and coming reality. Vision looks beyond the obvious to the actual. Peter is writing about the "vision of faith" (1:8). Faith enables a person to love someone and believe in someone who has never been seen. The word *faith* in its noun, verb and adjective forms appears over 500 times in the New Testament. The frequency of its usage mandates a deeper understanding of its meaning. My independent master's project involved the study of every occurrence of this strategic word in both the English translations and the Greek versions of the New Testament. After investing more than eighty hours of research to define faith correctly, I came up with the following definition: "Faith is the fully confident attitude and inevitably obedient action in response to the demands of God, who has exhibited His trustworthiness, for a complete consecration of self and possessions." You would expect such a prolonged verbosity from a seminary student! A.W. Tozer's definition is even longer:

> Faith, as the Bible knows it, is confidence in God and His Son Jesus Christ; it is the response of the soul to the divine character as revealed in the Scriptures; and even this response is impossible apart from the prior inworking of the Holy Spirit. Faith is a gift of God to a penitent soul and has nothing whatsoever to do with the senses or data they can afford.[15]

Hebrews 11:1 declares that "faith is being sure of what we hope for and certain of what we do not see." Faith is confidence derived from spiritual eyesight rather than confidence derived from sensory vision.

Peter was present when Jesus taught Thomas the meaning of faith (see John 20:24-29). One week before this lesson took place, Thomas had missed the meeting between Jesus and His disciples. Because he did not have sensory evidence he refused to believe. In John 20:25 he expresses his uncertainty: "Unless I see the nail marks in his hands . . . and put my hand into his side, *I will not believe it*" (emphasis added). Seven days later his demands were met:

A week later his disciples were in the house again, and Thomas was with them. Though the doors were locked, Jesus came and stood among them and said, "Peace be with you!" Then he said to Thomas, "Put your finger here; see my hands. Reach out your hand and put it into my side. Stop doubting and believe." (20:26-27)

Immediately, Thomas responded with the affirmation, "My Lord and my God!" (20:28). He was tardy in his faith response, and Jesus applauded another type of response which dovetails with Peter's description of faith: "Then Jesus told him, 'Because you have seen me, you have believed; blessed are those who have not seen and yet have believed' " (20:29). The blessing is in the believing *before the seeing!* This brand of faith results in a believer who is filled with love and inexpressible and glorious joy. The promise is possessed by the suffering saint, and there comes an empowerment to love, even without all the sensory evidence, and to rejoice despite the circumstances and liabilities. The cup is full and running over, so much so that the joy is *beyond definition*. This is not a joy reserved for heaven but a joy which is an existential reality, a present tense possession.

And the goal of the faith is being realized in the present life. One writer illuminates the concept of the objective being achieved with this insight:

> The "goal" *(telos)* or consummation of faith is the "salvation of your souls." No soul-and-body dichotomy of Greek thought is implied. The "soul" is used in the Semitic biblical sense of "self" or "person." Therefore the thought of this section closes with the believers' enjoyment of the future salvation in this present age.[16]

Even in this world the Christian is "under the spout where the glory comes out"!

Revealed More Than Prophets (1:10-12)

The prophets play a significant role in God's disclosure of the plan of salvation. In theology class the student is taught that four major lights illuminate God's plan for man, namely, nature, the Law, the prophets and Jesus Christ. Peter highlights the contribution of the prophets in declaring God's grace to a fallen race. It is interesting to note that although they declared this grace, they were not able to decode and decipher the time and the circumstances of Christ's suffering and His glory. They "searched intently" is a strong expression of passionate effort to discover truth.

Peter is encouraging his readers with an incredible thought—the prophets in their "grace chase," in their assiduous attempts to pinpoint the time and details of the Messiah, did not grasp the understanding of Jesus Christ and His grace as did the believers who lived during the post-ascension era. These scattered saints had obtained an incredible advantage: they had hindsight while the prophets had only foresight. A superintendent of a holiness denomination is reported to have once said: "If my foresight was like my hindsight, I'd be *out of sight!*" The esteemed prophets had served these believers (1:12) and built a platform of understanding that would permit their spiritual descendants to realize a fuller view of Jesus Christ than they did. Those first-century saints and, by extension, the saints of our modern era, stand upon the shoulders of the prophets.

This prophetic ministry to future generations of believers is a distinct honor. Peter inflates the privilege of these believers by stating, "Even angels long to look into these things" (1:12). Apparently, angels do not experience this revelation as those who have been redeemed from sin. Can you imagine that angels are envious of Christians' access to the grace of Jesus Christ? The phrase "long to look" from the Greek word *parakupto,* conveys the image of a person bending over and stooping down to look at something or someone of great interest. This word appears in Luke 24:12 to describe the author's bending down to survey the linens of Jesus in the empty tomb, and it is employed in John 20:11 to depict Mary's bending down to look into the vacancy that Jesus had left in that same tomb. The prophets of old and the angels did not have the "reserved seats" that these believers boasted of in the first century. This scattered band of believers had the instruments to form a "praise band" because of what God had done for them in history.

Conclusion

The shallow pond is much more vulnerable to evaporation than the *deep river*. Likewise, the shallow Christian life is much more vulnerable than the *deeper Christian life*. The more intimate a believer is with God, the more capable he or she is of surviving a hostile environment. The pursuit of God enables a person to utilize such intangibles as faith, hope and love to advantage. These first-century Christians would have been crushed if they operated on empirical evidence. However, Peter summons them to a dynamic faith which gazes upon the faithfulness of God, who can even convert the fire of life's toughest trials into a refining instrument to develop battle-hardened soldiers for His service.

Discussion Questions for Further Study

1. What are some "hope factors" for you in times of suffering?

2. Name some occasions when the heavenly Father used the refiner's fire in your life or the lives of others.

3. What biblical character do you think of when you hear the words "the refiner's fire"?

4. What is your definition of faith?

5. What advantages and disadvantages are there to living in this era of church history?

Endnotes

1 A.B. Simpson, *Days of Heaven on Earth* (Camp Hill, PA: Christian Publications, 1984), June 5.

2 William Barclay, *The Letters of James and Peter, The Daily Study Bible Series*, Vol. 14 (Philadelphia: Westminster Press, 1976), 171.

3 There are several Greek words used to convey mercy in the New Testament, but the primary Greek word for this concept, *eleos*, appears here. Vine describes the term in this fashion, "*eleos* is the outward manifestation of pity; it assumes need on the part of him who receives it, and resources adequate to meet the need on the part of him who shows it."—W.E. Vine, *Expository Dictionary of New Testament Words*, 4 vols. (Grand Rapids, MI: Zondervan, 1952), Vol. 3:60.

4 A.W. Tozer, *The Knowledge of the Holy* (San Francisco: Harper & Row, 1961), 90.

5 Joseph Addison, cited in Ibid., 93.

6 Present active participle of *zao*.—Archibald Thomas Robertson, *Word Pictures in the New Testament, The General Epistles and The Revelation of John*, Vol. 6 (Grand Rapids, MI: Baker, 1933), 81.

7 A.B. Simpson, *The Epistles of Peter, John and Jude* (Harrisburg, PA: Christian Publications, n.d.), 7-8.

8 Warren W. Wiersbe, *Be Hopeful* (Wheaton, IL: Scripture Press, 1982), 21.

9 Colin Brown, gen. ed., *The New International Dictionary*

of New Testament Theology, 3 vols. (Grand Rapids, MI: Zondervan Publishing, 1979), Vol. 3:215.

10 E. Stanley Jones, *Abundant Living* (Nashville, TN: Abingdon Press, 1942), 54.

11 Harold L. Fickett, Jr., *Peter's Principles* (Ventura, CA: Regal Books, 1974), 24.

12 Billy Graham, *World Aflame* (Minneapolis, MN: Billy Graham Evangelistic Association, 1965), xiii.

13 Leon Morris et. al., *Hebrews-Revelation, The Expositor's Bible Commentary*, Vol. 12, ed. Frank E. Gaebelein (Grand Rapids, MI: Zondervan, 1981), 221.

14 George Barna, *The Power of Vision* (Ventura, CA: Regal Books, 1992), 28.

15 A.W. Tozer, *Renewed Day by Day*, Vol. 1 (Camp Hill, PA: Christian Publications, 1980), September 6.

16 Morris et. al., *Hebrews-Revelation*, 221.

3

The Imperative of Holiness

1 Peter 1:13-25

Therefore, prepare your minds for action; be self-controlled; set your hope fully on the grace to be given you when Jesus Christ is revealed. As obedient children, do not conform to the evil desires you had when you lived in ignorance. But just as he who called you is holy, so be holy in all you do; for it is written: "Be holy, because I am holy."

Since you call on a Father who judges each man's work impartially, live your lives as strangers here in reverent fear. For you know that it was not with perishable things such as silver or gold that you were redeemed from the empty way of life handed down to you from your forefathers, but with the precious blood of Christ, a lamb without blemish or defect. He was chosen before the creation of the world, but was re-

*vealed in these last times for your sake. Through
him you believe in God, who raised him from the
dead and glorified him, and so your faith and
hope are in God.*

*Now that you have purified yourselves by
obeying the truth so that you have sincere love
for your brothers, love one another deeply, from
the heart. For you have been born again, not of
perishable seed, but of imperishable, through the
living and enduring word of God. For,*

> *"All men are like grass,
>   and all their glory is like the flowers of
>   the field;
> the grass withers and the flowers fall,
>   but the word of the Lord stands forever."*

*And this is the word that was preached to you.
(1 Peter 1:13-25)*

MEDIOCRITY IS NOT THE ACCEPTABLE
level of performance for the Christian.
Peter did not find it acceptable in the
first century either, and he addresses his audience
next with the *imperative of holiness.* He is challenging them to be transported to the highlands of
spiritual, moral and ethical triumph. He is calling
them and us from the lowlands of spiritual mediocrity. Herbert Schlossberg fired this painful assessment in his book *Idols for Destruction:*
"Protestantism has largely divested itself of the

transcendent and has become almost indistinguishable from the surrounding culture."[1] This is a sad commentary on the state of the Church and its constituents. The dynamic disciples of Jesus Christ should be a counterculture to those who are living apart from Jesus Christ; they should manifest a contrast, not a conformity, to those who are lost. The distinction is less clear, the demarcation less precise between those who are "in Christ" and those who are "outside Christ." The mist and fog have settled and the darkness and light are beginning to merge into a disappointing gray. Tozer assessed modern Christianity in these terms:

> In many churches Christianity has been watered down until the solution is so weak that if it were poison it would not hurt anyone, and if it were medicine it would not cure anyone!
>
> Now I want to bring you my postulate that most present-day Christians live sub-Christian lives.
>
> I repeat: Most modern Christians live sub-Christian lives!
>
> Most Christians are not joyful persons because they are not holy persons, and they are not holy persons because they are not filled with the Holy Spirit, and they are not filled with the Holy Spirit because they are not separated persons.
>
> The Spirit cannot fill whom He cannot separate, and whom He cannot fill, He can-

not make holy, and whom He cannot make holy, He cannot make happy!²

The Holy Expectation (1:13-16)

Peter's clarion call to holy living begins in 1:13. The apostle has articulated in the first twelve verses the salvation which has been achieved through the grace of God and the sacrifice of Jesus Christ. Some of the benefits of salvation have been clearly defined. Now, because the recipient has been placed into God's family and has been endowed with incredible dividends from such a relationship, a prescribed lifestyle is the reasonable expectation.

The phrase "prepare your minds for action" or the KJV's more graphic translation, "gird up the loins of your minds," conveys a particular image. This word picture has been elaborated in this manner:

In the east men wore long flowing robes which hindered fast progress or strenuous action. Round the waist they wore a broad belt or girdle; and when strenuous action was necessary they shortened the long robe by pulling it up within the belt in order to give them freedom of movement. The English equivalent of the phrase would be to roll up one's sleeves or to take off one's jacket. Peter is telling his people that they must be ready for the most strenuous mental en-

deavor. They must never be content with a
flabby and unexamined faith; they must set
to and think things out and think them
through. It may be that they will have to
discard some things.[3]

In short, tuck in what will slow you down and
position yourself to run the race that God has designed for you.

Self-Control

Another trait of a saved life is a self-controlled
demeanor.[4] Proverbs 25:28 declares: "Like a city
whose walls are broken down is a man who lacks
self-control." Paul makes self-control an issue in
the selection of elders for church leadership in
First Timothy 3:2, and he includes it as the final
evidence of the fruit of the Spirit in Galatians
5:23.

Peter will incorporate self-control two other
times in his first letter. These verses express this
virtue's strategic importance for Christian living
(emphasis added):

The end of all things is near. Therefore be
clear minded and *self-controlled* so that you
can pray. (4:7)

Be *self-controlled* and alert. Your enemy the
devil prowls around like a roaring lion looking for someone to devour. (5:8)

Look Beyond the Present

The third act of the Christian is to look beyond the present to the "grace to be given you when Jesus Christ is revealed." The Christian takes an eschatological rather than an existential view of circumstances. The consummation of the kingdom will be punctuated with the return of Jesus Christ, who will complete the benefit package of salvation. The definitive verse of Peter's letter is 5:12 which encompasses the reason for this literary production: "With the help of Silas, whom I regard as a faithful brother, I have written to you briefly, encouraging you and testifying that this is the true grace of God. Stand fast in it."

God's grace is the fixation point for the Christian's hopes and aspirations. Grace can be traced to the present everyday life of the Christian, but the final and glorious denouement provides a compelling incentive to live a consistent and consecrated life of holiness! "The best is yet to be," wrote Browning. May that be the truth of our Christian hope.[5] In the middle of frustrating days and long nights, authentic believers can rest their weary heads on this pillow of comfort: "The best is yet to come!"

Obedience

Peter returns to the issue of obedience as he sets the table for the main course on the *imperative of holiness*. He employs the analogy of children, which is a recurrent concept in the imagery of the redeemed in the New Testament. Paul, John and Peter—all of these men incorporated children into their writings. There are compliant children and there are defiant children, and Peter is stressing that the former, not the latter, is the function of God's sons and daughters. These children are to be transformed by their faith and not conformed to the evil desires which occupied their pursuits prior to conversion.

Paul emphasized this counterculture lifestyle in Romans 12:1-2:

> Therefore, I urge you, brothers, in view of God's mercy, to offer your bodies as living sacrifices, holy and pleasing to God— this is your spiritual act of worship. Do not conform any longer to the pattern of this world, but be transformed by the renewing of your mind. Then you will be able to test and approve what God's will is—his good, pleasing and perfect will.

The people of God were to be distinguished from the society in which they lived. God's children were to be easily recognized for their adherence to God's Word, God's will and God's way!

The contrary conjunction *but* of First Peter 1:15 pivots the discussion to a crystal-clear call to holiness.

God is holy! He is described as a holy God more often than He is described as a just, righteous or loving God. *Holiness is the primary attribute of God.*

What do we mean by the word *holy*? The primary Hebrew word for "to be holy" or "to make holy" is *kadesh.*[6] The predominant view of the root meaning for *kadesh* and its derivatives is "to set apart or distinguish." It is a word which communicates contrast. It is a word often utilized to describe God, for He is above all else, separate from His creation and perfectly pure, without blemish or flaw.

A study of the Greek word *hagiazo,* the word used in the Septuagint to translate *kadesh,* demonstrates that in the New Testament there is a renewed emphasis on God as holy, and there is an expanded view of man as designed to function as a holy representative of God. The verb *hagiazo* appears twenty-eight times in the New Testament. It has residency in thirteen of the twenty-seven books in the New Testament.

Peter quotes from the book of Leviticus in 1:16. There are four references, in particular, that address this command to "be holy." They are recorded as follows (emphasis added):

I am the LORD your God; consecrate yourselves and be *holy,* because I am *holy.* Do not make yourselves unclean by any creature that moves about on the ground. (Leviticus 11:44)

I am the LORD who brought you up out of Egypt to be your God; therefore be *holy,* because I am *holy.* (11:45)

Speak to the entire assembly of Israel and say to them: "Be *holy* because I, the LORD your God, am *holy.*" (19:2)

Consecrate yourselves and be *holy,* because I am the LORD your God. (20:7)

Peter anchors the call to Christian holiness to the reality of God's holiness. This is the same nexus that the Levitical writer made in all four of the verses quoted above. A twentieth-century book makes the same assertion:

This call to a holy life is based on the fact that God Himself is holy. Because God is holy, He requires that we be holy. Many Christians have what we might call a "cultural holiness." They adapt to the character and behavior pattern of Christians around them. As the Christian culture around them is more or less holy, so these Christians are more or less holy. But God has not called us to be like those around us. He has called us to be like Himself. Holiness is nothing less than conformity to the character of God.[7]

Where are the men and women whose morality reflects God's holiness, whose light shines in darkness, whose fragrance fills a stench-filled room, whose lives are a counterculture to the world which operates from a non-theistic ethic?

There has been too much clinging to the cosmos and not enough cleavage from its worldview and lifestyles. The call to separation, to the "peculiar people" mode, has for many lost its bite. In *The Pursuit of God*, A.W. Tozer hoists this red flag: "Now we have reached a low place of sand and burnt wire grass and worst of all, we have made the Word of God conform to our experience and accepted this low plane as the very pasture of the blessed."[8]

As God issued a call for Israel to be a counter-culture in the pre-occupation days, He still longs for His people to "be holy as I am holy."

The apostle Paul understood the expectation to be holy. In First Corinthians 4:16 he stated, "Therefore I urge you to imitate me." Later in that same letter he tendered this imperative, "Follow my example, as I follow the example of Christ" (11:1). It may seem boastful, but Paul believed that his life's mission was *to make the invisible Christ visible*. It should be a part not only of *his* personal mission statement, but it should be a significant part of every Christian's personal mission statement.

The Holy Lamb (1:17-21)

Peter incorporates the fatherhood of God into his appeal for authentic Christian living. The Old Testament included references to God as Father, but these few occurrences refer to corporate ("we"), not individual, relationships and lack the familial and intimate emphasis that is resident in

the New Testament. A multi-faceted portrait of
the personality of God emerges from His role as
Father. His compassion, His benevolent approach
to His children, His forgiving nature as a spiritual
parent are byproducts of the heavenly Father's
functions. J.I. Packer made this assertion regarding the fatherhood of God and its impact on spiritual life:

> You sum up the whole of the New Testa-
> ment teaching in a single phrase, if you
> speak of it as a revelation of the Fatherhood
> of the holy Creator. In the same way, you
> sum up the whole of New Testament reli-
> gion if you describe it as the knowledge of
> God as one's holy Father. If you want to
> judge how well a person understands Chris-
> tianity, find out how much he makes of the
> thought of being God's child, and having
> God as his Father. If this is not the thought
> that prompts and controls his worship and
> prayers and his whole outlook on life, it
> means that he does not understand Christi-
> anity very well at all. For everything that
> Christ taught, everything that makes the
> New Testament new, and better than the
> Old, everything that is distinctively Chris-
> tian as opposed to merely Jewish, is summed
> up in the knowledge of the Fatherhood of
> God. "Father" is the Christian name for
> God.[9]

Peter adds to our understanding of God's fatherhood by informing his readers that this role encompasses His judgmental character. Fathers must judge, and their judgment must be impartial. The New Testament affirms this concept of impartial judgment in the following two verses: "For God does not show favoritism" (Romans 2:11); "My brothers, as believers in our glorious Lord Jesus Christ, don't show favoritism" (James 2:1).

In view of the Father's impartial, "no favors" approach to judgment, the child of God is summoned to live as a stranger (see 1 Peter 1:1; 1:17) in this present world. Peter inserts this "stranger" theme to sharpen the focus of the believer as he or she walks in this world, for the child of God is an alien whose citizenship is in the commonwealth of heaven! The word for *here* in 1:17 is derived from the Greek word *paroikia* and means "a temporary visit in a foreign land."[10] The destiny of the Christian is beyond this planet which circles the sun; the hope of the Christian is elevated higher than earth's atmosphere; the rewards of the Christian are being deposited in God's heaven. Therefore, the Christian is to be uncomfortable and dissatisfied by the earthly habitat and is to live as one representing another country and another King!

Peter attaches to this "sojourner" mode of living the idea of reverent fear. The word for *fear* is from the Greek word *phobos* from which we carve out the English word *phobia*. The believer possesses a reverent phobia because, as Barclay reminds us,

"Reverence is the attitude of mind of the man who is always aware that he is in the presence of God."[11]

It is crucial that Christians not allow their self-consciousness to dictate their attitude.

Because of a fallen world, those who identify with Jesus find themselves often judged with prejudice. Sometimes a college professor is unjustifiably harsh in grading a Christian's paper because the student has a variant worldview. Sometimes an employer overlooks a believer for an anticipated promotion, perhaps due to a stand which the believer has endorsed in the workplace. An athletic coach may not grasp why a player cannot participate on Sundays, and therefore that young man or woman is discounted and devalued, even though there is sufficient athletic talent and desire to play a positive role on the team. Peter's inspired counsel is preparation for these scenarios and bids the one who is treated with negative partiality to remember that God will be the final judge, and He will judge with impeccable impartiality.

The apostle Peter anchors the believer's holy and counterculture lifestyle to the *redemptive* work of the precious Lamb of God, Jesus Christ. The verb for *redeemed* in 1:18 is in the passive voice, which indicates that our redemption did not involve our personal participation. Another had to administer the process which involves a payment. The biblical definition centers on a release or emancipation which is secured by the

payment of a ransom. Edwin Blum illuminates
the circumstances of redemption during the Roman Empire:

> The Greek word *lytroo (redeem)* goes back to
> the institution of slavery in ancient Rome.
> Any representative first-century church
> would have three kinds of members: slaves,
> freemen, and freed men. People became
> slaves in various ways—through war, bank-
> ruptcy, sale by themselves, sale by parents,
> or by birth. Slaves could normally look for-
> ward to freedom after a certain period of
> service and often after the payment of a
> price. Money to buy this freedom could be
> earned by the slave in his spare time or by
> doing more than his owner required. Often
> the price could be provided by someone else.
> By the payment of a price *(lytron, antilytron)*,
> a person could be set free from his bondage
> or servitude. A freed man was a person who
> formerly had been a slave, but was now re-
> deemed.[12]

What is the price? Peter replaces the what with
a Who! The agent of redemption was the Lamb of
God, Jesus Christ. When John saw Jesus coming
at Bethany on the other side of the Jordan, he exclaimed, "Look, *the Lamb of God*, who takes away
the sin of the world!" (John 1:29, emphasis
added). The Baptizer foreshadowed Jesus as the
sacrificial Lamb who would atone for the sins of

the world. Paul wrote in the first chapter of Ephesians concerning Jesus' blood and its significance for the redeemed, "In him we have redemption through his blood, the forgiveness of sins, in accordance with the riches of God's grace" (1:7). And John's remarkable vision in Revelation embraces a Lamb and the song sung in the Lamb's honor:

> Then I saw a Lamb, looking as if it had been slain, standing in the center of the throne, encircled by the four living creatures and the elders. He had seven horns and seven eyes, which are the seven spirits of God sent out into all the earth. He came and took the scroll from the right hand of him who sat on the throne. And when he had taken it, the four living creatures and the twenty-four elders fell down before the Lamb. Each one had a harp and they were holding golden bowls full of incense, which are the prayers of the saints. And they sang a new song:
>
> "You are worthy to take the scroll
>   and to open its seals,
> because you were slain,
>   and with your blood you purchased
>   men for God
>   from every tribe and language and people and nation.
>   (Revelation 5:6-9)

A.W. Tozer, writing of the glory of the cross and the Christ of the cross, said:

> Never make any mistake about this—the suffering of Jesus on the cross was not punitive! It was not for Himself and not for punishment of anything that He Himself had done.
>
> The suffering of Jesus was corrective. He was willing to suffer in order that He might correct us and perfect us.
>
> Brethren, that is the glory of the cross! . . .
>
> It began in His wounds and ended in our purification!
>
> It began in His bruises and ended in our cleansing!
>
> That painful and acute conviction that accompanies repentance may well subside and a sense of peace and cleansing come, but even the holiest of justified men will think back over his part in the wounding and chastisement of the Lamb of God.
>
> A sense of shock will come over him!
>
> A sense of wonder will remain—wonder that the Lamb that was wounded should turn his wounds into the cleansing and forgiveness of one who wounded Him![13]

The redemptive exchange did not utilize silver and gold, perishable and finite collectibles. This transaction involved the visible picture of the invisible God. This transaction meant that God would be crucified. This transaction meant a Healer would be wounded!

Jesus Christ delivered us from our empty way of life (1 Peter 1:18-19). Fickett notes that the word for *empty, mataios,* actually means "striving for something that is never achieved."[14] The unblemished Lamb restored the lost sheep. His fullness countered our emptiness; His supply satisfied our demand; His perfection replaced our imperfection! Charles Wesley's classic hymn, "Arise, My Soul, Arise!" begins with these words:

> Arise, my soul, arise!
> Shake off thy guilty fears;
> The bleeding Sacrifice
> In my behalf appears.
> Before the throne my Surety stands,
> Before the throne my Surety stands:
> My name is written on His hands.

The story is told, in a variety of versions, concerning a boy that had made his own boat. He took it down to the water's edge, placed it in the waves and watched it sail away. He tried to retrieve it, but he was unable to get it back. One day as he rode his bicycle past a storefront window, he noticed his boat displayed in the window. When he approached the proprietor, the man told him that the boat would cost him $3. Frustrated, he went home to tell his father, who upon hearing the story helped him devise a plan to earn the money. Eventually, $3 in hand, he returned to the store and handed the $3 to the proprietor. As he did, he made this remark, "I made it, I lost it and I bought it back!"

So it is with all of the redeemed of the Lord— He made them, and when sin led them into spiritual bankruptcy and lostness, *He bought them back*. He bought them back!

The Holy Word (1:22-25)

The apostle's call to holy living concludes with an energetic endorsement of the imperishable Word of God. In 1:22 obedience and the Word are integrated and the result is twofold: purification and the love of the brothers.

Obedience has already been established by Peter as one of the nonnegotiables of the elect (1:15). It surfaces again and is inextricably linked to purification, "[purifying] yourselves by obeying the truth" (1:22). Therefore, obedience is not only a byproduct of salvation and sanctification, it is one of the raw materials. As the individual obeys the Word of God, he or she experiences the *truth that transforms*. Andrew Murray wrote in *The New Life*, "With a servant, a warrior, a child, a subject, obedience is indispensable, the first token of integrity."[15] When the seeker moves beyond just hearing or acknowledging the truth and takes the next step, actually complying with the truth, a beautiful series of developments begin to emerge.

A second byproduct of obeying the truth is evident in the love that is expressed for the brothers in the family of God. The authentic Christian must possess both a "vertical" love for God *and* a "horizontal" love for the Church. Jesus Christ explicitly addressed this phenomenon in His pre-crucifixion address to the disciples: "A new command I give you: Love one another. As I have loved you, so you must love one another. By this all men will know that you are my disciples, if you love one another" (John 13:34-35).

The badge of discipleship for the Christian is the love which is expressed to the brothers and sisters of God's family. Peter accents this dimension of love and urges that it be "deeply, from the heart" (1 Peter 1:22). Charles Colson illustrated this love for all the saints in his autobiography *Born Again.* After he had been imprisoned for his role in the Watergate scandal, Colson's faith was severely challenged. His wife was suspicious of this "born-again" experience and his son was picked up on drug charges. Colson's confidence in the Christian faith began to deteriorate. Several Christians in Washington, including Senators Hatfield, Hughes and Quie, participated in a prayer ministry to support him. Senator Quie discovered a "dusty" law that permitted an innocent man to serve a prison term for the guilty man. When Quie came forward and volunteered to complete Colson's prison term, the prisoner, though he turned down the offer, vividly witnessed the "love of saint for saint."[16]

Peter links the new birth or born-again experience with the Word *(logos)* of God. This living and abiding Word brings to the dead in sin the very breath of life! The revelation of God, natural, prophetic, spoken, written and *incarnate* in Jesus Christ comprises this imperishable, never dying, indestructible seed. This living quality is expressed in Hebrews 4:12: "For the word of God is living and active. Sharper than any double-edged sword, it penetrates even to dividing soul and spirit, joints and marrow; it judges the thoughts and attitudes of the heart."

The Word of God penetrates the soil of the heart and germinates, resulting in new life and fruitful growth! This is a fruit-bearing God, for life begets life. This emphasis does not diminish or detract from the instrumentality of the Holy Spirit in the new birth (Titus 3:5); rather, it highlights the instrumentality of God's Word in the equation. James 1:18 confirms this deduction: "He chose to give us birth through the word of truth, that we might be a kind of firstfruits of all he created."

In the final two verses of the chapter, Peter contrasts the mortality of man and his glory with the immortality of God's Word. The apostle quotes from Isaiah 40:6-8. One expositor supplies this enlightening commentary on the quotation:

> The quotation comes from the "Book of Comfort" in Isaiah as the prophetic message of God to an exiled and oppressed people. How fitting the application is to pilgrim Christians (cf. 1 Peter 1:1) in the light of their oppression by the pagan world. . . . The theme of Isaiah's prophecy is the per-

ishable nature of all flesh and the imperishable nature of the Word of God.[17]

The Word of God is *always resilient, always relevant!*

Conclusion

As Peter issued a call for the first-century
Christians to be separated from their culture and
reflect the purity and power of their God and Jesus Christ His Son, so today's disciples are to put
holiness on their daily agenda! Holiness is the
drumbeat of the Christian of any age in any age.
Oswald Chambers issues this noble challenge:

Continually restate to yourself what the purpose of your life is. The destined end of an
individual is not happiness, not health, but
holiness.

The one thing that matters most is
whether a person will accept the God who
will make him holy. At all costs one must be
rightly related to God.

Do I believe I need to be holy? Do I believe God can come into me and make me
holy?

God has one destined end for humans—
holiness. He is not an eternal "blessing ma-
chine" for people. He did not come to save
people out of pity; he came to save people
because he had created them to be holy.[18]

The manifestation of holiness by humanity cannot be synthetically produced. The holy or sanctified life must be implemented by the prevailing
presence of the Holy Spirit. A.W. Tozer prescribes these steps in his small but significant book
How to Be Filled with the Holy Spirit:

> Here is how to receive [the Holy Spirit].
> First, present your body to Him (Romans
> 12:1-2). God can't fill what He can't have.
> Now I ask you: Are you ready to present
> your body with all its functions and all that
> it contains—your mind, your personality,
> your spirit, your love, your ambitions, your
> all? That is the first thing. That is a simple,
> easy act—presenting the body. Are you will-
> ing to do it?
>
> Now the second thing is to ask (Luke
> 11:9-11), and I set aside all theological objec-
> tions to this text. They say that is not for to-
> day. Well, why did the Lord leave it in the
> Bible then? Why didn't He put it some-
> where else; why did He put it where I could
> see it if He didn't want me to believe it? It is
> all for us, and if the Lord wanted to do it,
> He could give it without our asking, but He
> chooses to have us ask. "Ask of me, and I
> will give thee" is always God's order; so
> why not ask?
>
> Acts 5:32 tells us the third thing to do.
> God gives His Holy Spirit to them that
> obey Him. Are you ready to obey and do

what you are asked to do? What would that be? Simply to live by the Scriptures as you understand them. Simple, but revolutionary.

The next thing is have faith (Galatians 3:2). We receive Him by faith as we receive the Lord in salvation by faith. He comes as a gift of God to us in power. First He comes in some degree and measure when we are converted. Without Him we couldn't be born again, because we are born of the Spirit. But I am talking about something different now, an advance over that. I am talking about His coming and possessing the full body and mind and life and heart, taking the whole personality over, gently, but directly and bluntly, and making it His, so that we may become a habitation of God through the Spirit.[19]

When men and women pursue God, when men and women bring to Him an open vessel and ask Him to fill it, when men and women comprehend that He is the potter and they are the clay, when men and women radiate holiness and display Christlikeness, then a renewal movement will sweep over our churches, and if enough churches join in, then a renewal movement will sweep over our communities, and if enough communities join in, then a renewal movement will sweep over our states, and if enough states join in, then a renewal movement will spread over our nation. Acts 2 is an historical account of what happens when people are filled with the Spirit and when God's priorities become humans' priorities.

Charles Finney, one of the giants in the history of revival in America, made this prediction and follows it with some significant inquiries:

> One holy church crucified to the world would do more to promote Christianity than all the churches in the country, living as they do now. If I had strength to go through the churches, I would preach to bring them up to the standard of holy living. Of what use is it to convert sinners and make them such Christians as these? Of what use is it to try to convert sinners and make them feel that there is something in religion, and then by your conformity to the world prove that there is nothing in it?
>
> Where shall the Lord look for a church—like the first Church—that will be separate and serve God?
>
> Do you believe that God commands you not to be conformed to the world? Do you believe it? And dare you obey it, regardless of what people say about you? Will you separate yourself from the world and never again be controlled by its principles and practices? Will you do it?[20]

Discussion Questions for Further Study

1. How do you define the word *holiness*?

2. Find some verses which support the premise that God's expectation for each believer is holiness.

3. What can a believer do to pursue holiness or the deeper life?

4. What do you think of this statement: "Every child of God is called to 'make the invisible Christ visible' "?

5. How are you utilizing the Word of God in your personal life?

Endnotes

1 Herbert Schlossberg, *Idols for Destruction* (Nashville, TN: Thomas Nelson, 1983), 238.

2 A.W. Tozer, *I Talk Back to the Devil* (Camp Hill, PA: Christian Publications, 1990), 31.

3 William Barclay, *The Letters of James and Peter, The Daily Study Bible Series*, Vol. 14 (Philadelphia: Westminster Press, 1976), 183.

4 " 'Be self-controlled' renders the Greek present participle *nephontes* and implies another figure. The original meaning of *nepho* related to abstaining from excessive use of wine. In the NT its sense broadens to 'live soberly'—a meaning that embraces sound judgment in all areas of life."—Leon Morris et. al., *Hebrews-Revelation, The Expositor's Bible Commentary*, Vol. 12, ed. Frank E. Gaebelein (Grand Rapids, MI: Zondervan, 1981), 223.

5 Robert Browning, "Rabbi Ben Ezra," Stanza 1, 1864.

6 The word *kadesh* is applied across a wide spectrum. It is applied to places such as *holy ground* (Exodus 3:4-5) and *holy camp* (Exodus 29:14). It is employed in regard to things, such as the *holy linen coat* of Aaron and his *holy*

garments (Leviticus 16:4). This designation is applied to *fruit* (Leviticus 19:24), *vessels* (2 Chronicles 5:5, KJV) and *oil* (Psalm 89:20). The word is utilized in respect to times and observances, eg. the *seventh day*, which is holy (Genesis 2:3) and a *fast* is holy (Joel 1:14).

7 Jerry Bridges, *The Pursuit of Holiness* (Colorado Springs, CO: NavPress, 1978), 25-26.

8 A.W. Tozer, *The Pursuit of God* (Camp Hill, PA: Christian Publications, 1982), 70.

9 J.I. Packer, *Knowing God* (Downers Grove, IL: InterVarsity Press, 1973), 182.

10 Harold L. Fickett, Jr., *Peter's Principles* (Ventura, CA: Regal Books, 1974), 44.

11 Barclay, *The Daily Study Bible*, 188.

12 Morris et. al., *Hebrews-Revelation*, 224-225.

13 A.W. Tozer, *Renewed Day by Day, Vol 1* (Camp Hill, PA: Christian Publications, 1980), August 13.

14 Fickett, *Peter's Principles*, 46.

15 Andrew Murray, *The New Life*, quoted in Elisabeth Elliot, *A Lamp for My Feet* (Ann Arbor, MI: Servant Publications, 1985), 33.

16 Charles Colson, *Born Again* (Old Tappan, NJ: Revell, 1976), 338-339.

17 Morris et. al., *Hebrews-Revelation*, 227.

18 Oswald Chambers, *My Utmost for His Highest* (Old Tappan, NJ: Revell, 1935), 403-404.

19 A.W. Tozer, *How to Be Filled with the Holy Spirit* (Camp Hill, PA: Christian Publications, n.d.), 47-48.

20 Charles G. Finney, *Crystal Christianity* (Pittsburgh, PA: Whitaker House, 1985), 159.

4

The Imperative to Assume a Christian Identity

1 Peter 2:1-10

Therefore, rid yourselves of all malice and all deceit, hypocrisy, envy, and slander of every kind. Like newborn babies, crave pure spiritual milk, so that by it you may grow up in your salvation, now that you have tasted that the Lord is good.

As you come to him, the living Stone—rejected by men but chosen by God and precious to him—you also, like living stones, are being built into a spiritual house to be a holy priesthood, offering spiritual sacrifices acceptable to God through Jesus Christ. For in Scripture it says:

"See, I lay a stone in Zion,
a chosen and precious cornerstone,
and the one who trusts in him
will never be put to shame."

*Now to you who believe, this stone is precious.
But to those who do not believe,*

> *"The stone the builders rejected
> has become the capstone,"*

and,

> *"A stone that causes men to stumble
> and a rock that makes them fall."*

*They stumble because they disobey the message—
which is also what they were destined for.*

*But you are a chosen people, a royal priest-
hood, a holy nation, a people belonging to God,
that you may declare the praises of him who
called you out of darkness into his wonderful
light. Once you were not a people, but now you
are the people of God; once you had not received
mercy, but now you have received mercy. (1 Peter 2:1-10)*

THERE IS A LEGEND ABOUT a boy who
was raised by coyotes. He fell out of a
covered wagon in the prairie country of
the American West. Adopted by a pack of these
scavengers, the boy, later called Pecos Bill, grew
up howling at the moon, running on his hands and
knees and feeding on a coyote's diet. One day, a
cowboy discovered him and held up a mirror before his eyes and communicated to him that he

was a human being and not a wild animal. All those years he had been mistaken about his identity. Since he did not know who he was it was impossible for him to live as he was intended to live. Like Pecos Bill, unless we know who we are, we cannot function properly. Peter provides a plurality of analogies at the outset of chapter 2 which concretely convey the *identity of the Christian,* including the concepts of the Christian as a *newborn,* a *living stone* and a *priest.*

Newborns (2:1-3)

Peter has just broached the issue of being born again (1:23), and this means that a different lifestyle is in order. He begins by employing a forceful word in the original, *apotitheemi,* which communicates the idea of "putting away" or "shedding."[1] The believer cannot retain the negative aspects or traits of the old life if the new life is to be embraced and expressed with credibility. The apostle mentions a catalog of vices which the disciple must cast off, including malice, deceit, hypocrisy, envy and slander. A new birth demands a new life and these manifestations of darkness are accessories which are prohibited.

A newborn baby has no history. The chapters are yet to be written. The growth stages are many and varied. Nutrition is crucial! What are newborns to crave? The answer is found in 2:2: "pure spiritual milk." Oswald Sanders in writing about this passage includes the aspect of motherly care which must be exercised for the Christian in the nursery:

> The embryo life in the new believer is frag-
> ile and requires loving care and nurture in
> the dependent stage. A nursing mother is
> needed as long as the child remains a milk
> drinking infant. Gradually the child will
> progress to solid food as he or she moves on
> to adolescence.[2]

The community must look out for the newborns and infants. Every church must provide a
nursery! There must be an aggressive effort to
feed them the Bread of Life. Without the Word of
God, growth is short-term and fragile at best. The
leadership of the church must model a hunger and
thirst for the Word which is transmitted by example and results in the young children being favor-
ably disposed toward the healthy menu!

It is a sad sight when converts remain tiny
and frail for neglect of God's Word. Peter has
promoted passionately the imperishable Word at
the end of chapter 1, and he is endorsing its in-
take so that a church full of tiny children will
not be the result. The Word of God has been designed to supply the vitamins and minerals of
the faith.

The tasting analogy of 2:3, "now that you have
tasted," has affinity with Psalm 34:8, "Taste and
see that the LORD is good; blessed is the man who
takes refuge in him." It is important to remember

that this psalm is attributed to David when he was a fugitive prior to his ascension to the throne of Israel. Likewise, these believers that Peter was addressing found themselves amputated from their homeland. Yet David could sip the Lord and the readers of this letter could taste God's Word and be satisfied. The critical element in a Christian's situation is not location, but inspiration! The mobility of our times means that the contemporary Christian will be relocated and reassigned. His geography may change, but his diet may remain the same! In *The Pursuit of God*, A.W. Tozer concluded his first chapter with this powerful prayer which is drawn from the tasting aspect of a Christian's experience:

O God, I have tasted Thy goodness, and it has both satisfied me and made me thirsty for more. I am painfully conscious of my need of further grace. I am ashamed of my lack of desire. O God, the Triune God, I want to want Thee; I long to be filled with longing; I thirst to be made more thirsty still. Show me Thy glory, I pray Thee, so that I may know Thee indeed. Begin in mercy a new work of love within me. Say to my soul, "Rise up, my love, my fair one, and come away." Then give me grace to rise and follow Thee up from this misty lowland where I have wandered so long. In Jesus' Name, Amen.[3]

Spiritual food is essential for every Christian, but especially crucial to the new Christian. It is the responsibility of the shepherds in this person's life to provide a wholesome diet of God's Word. Perhaps we should ask the question, Are "the newborns in Jesus Christ" being fed properly? Religious junk food is not enough. A basic diet of God's Word is the answer to healthy growth. The tragic words of Milton should not apply to the new converts in our churches and families: "The hungry sheep look up, and are not fed."[4]

Living Stones (2:4-8)

Peter shifts his Christian analogy from a newborn to a stone—"living stones." He begins his metaphorical journey with the living Stone, Jesus Christ (2:4). The adjective *living* is coupled with other word pictures in the New Testament which describe Jesus' Messianic role. He is "the *living* bread that came down from heaven" (John 6:51, emphasis added). He dispenses *"living* water" (John 7:38, emphasis added). His body is "a new and *living* way" (Hebrews 10:20, emphasis added). Jesus Christ is a *living* Savior who sponsors a dynamic ministry through His people.

The apostle injects conflict into this concept by comparing God's disposition toward Christ, "chosen" and "precious," to man's rejection of Him. This is an extremely critical point for the elect of God who do the work of the kingdom. A believer can render service which is pleasing to God but which is ignored or devaluated by men. Christians should not expect non-Christians to be ecstatic about kingdom acts and ethics, because they have a different worldview and a different value system. This living Stone was precious to God and is priceless to those who have been ransomed by His, death and revitalized by His Spirit. But to those who do not understand Him or place faith in Him Jesus Christ is nothing more than an intruder who stifles their sinful lifestyle.

Peter proceeds to incorporate the believer into this analogy in 2:5: "You also, like living stones, are being built into a spiritual house." It must be remembered that the status of these Christians was one of dislocation. In the first verse of the letter, Peter used the word *diaspora* to refer to his readers. This word indicates that they were dispersed, scattered and exiled. The concept of being a living stone must have been appealing, for it speaks of connection and stability and purpose. They were a part of God's design; they did have a place; they were an important part of what He was building in this world. This spiritual household or temple is mentioned in other passages of Scripture (emphasis added), including:

Don't you know that you yourselves are God's *temple* and that God's Spirit lives in you? (1 Corinthians 3:16)

Consequently, you are no longer foreigners and aliens, but fellow citizens with God's people and members of God's *household*, built on the foundation of the apostles and prophets, with Christ Jesus himself as the chief cornerstone. In him the whole *building* is joined together and rises to become a holy *temple* in the Lord. And in him you too are being built together to become a dwelling in which God lives by his Spirit. (Ephesians 2:19-22)

John Stott, in his book *One People*, made this statement (emphasis added):

God's people are a *building* "not made with hands," a building which God is himself constructing, the rebuilt spiritual temple, with Jesus Christ as the only foundation as witnessed to by apostles and prophets, and the Holy Spirit as the Shechinah presence in the sanctuary.[5]

Peter then links this spiritual temple concept to the *priesthood of believers*. This is a natural transition from the temple to the priests that function within the temple. The first mention of this priesthood is found in Exodus 19:5-6, where Moses is instructed by God to declare to the people of Israel:

Now if you obey me fully and keep my covenant, then out of all nations you will be my treasured possession. Although the whole earth is mine, you will be for me a kingdom of priests and a holy nation. These

are the words you are to speak to the Israelites.

The priesthood of believers is not a doctrine
which originated in the New Testament or Reformation period. It is explicitly drawn from the Old
Testament during the Israelites' trek from Egypt
to the Promised Land.

One of the primary functions of the Old Testament priests was to administer the sacrifices and
offerings. This concept is updated and elevated in
the New Testament as the "priests" of God are
commanded to offer the sacrifice of their own
bodies (Romans 12:1), the sacrifice of their offerings (Philippians 4:18), sacrifices of praise (Hebrews 13:15) and sacrifices of good deeds
(Hebrews 13:16). The New Testament era does
not preempt the Christian from the role of the
priesthood. The sacrifices may be different, but
they are still imperative!

The last years of the twentieth century have
provided believers a window of opportunity to be
"priests" in the former Soviet Union. Missionaries
are entering this world power, which has now
been divided into many republics, and are discovering that it contains people in travail. Many of
these "priests" have left convenience and comfort
for inconvenience and hardship. Some of these
missionaries must sign a statement that they understand the risks of the environment because of
the nuclear disaster in Chernobyl. These brave
men and women must proclaim the Word of God

and the love of Christ to a suspicious and distrust-
ful audience. Nevertheless, they function as
priests, sacrificing so much so that other men and
women, who since World War II were venomous
enemies, can receive the peace and forgiveness of
Jesus Christ.

In verses 6-8, Peter stresses the theme, "Jesus is
the Cornerstone." He begins his examination by
quoting Isaiah 28:16: "So this is what the Sovereign
LORD says: 'See, I lay a stone in Zion, a tested stone,
a precious cornerstone for a sure foundation; the one
who trusts will never be dismayed.' "[6]

In the spiritual house which God is constructing, Jesus Christ serves as the chief Cornerstone.
All other living stones are measured by Him! Lari
Goss has written a popular song entitled "Cornerstone":

> Jesus is the Cornerstone,
> Came for sinners to atone;
> Though rejected by His own,
> He became the Cornerstone,
> Jesus is the Cornerstone.
> When I am by sin oppressed,
> On the Stone I am at rest,
> Where the seeds of truth are sown,
> He remains the Cornerstone,
> Jesus is the Cornerstone.[7]

The songwriter has captured the "divided
house" response which emerges from the person
and work of Jesus Christ.

Peter inserts Psalm 118:22 into his text: "The stone the builders rejected has become the cap-stone," and adds Isaiah 8:14:

. . . he will be
a stone that causes men to stumble
    and a rock that makes them fall.
And for the people of Jerusalem he will be
    a trap and a snare.

When Jesus Christ came He did not meet univer-sal acceptance; the same is true today. Jesus quoted Psalm 118:22 in Matthew 21:42 when He was confronting the chief priests and the Phari-sees. He was warning them that this Stone, which they were rejecting, would become a stone of judgment! All people choose whether they will obey and accept His gracious invitation to stand upon Him or refuse Him and be broken by this Cornerstone into many pieces.

The phrase "what they were destined for" in First Peter 2:8 whets the appetites of those who enjoy the Calvinist-Arminian debate.[8]

The central truth, the indispensable truth, is that the Lord Jesus Christ gives cohesion and pur-pose and value and beauty to the spiritual temple that God is constructing in this world!

Royal Priests (2:9-10)

First Peter 2:9 is one of the most significant verses in the New Testament. Four descriptions of the believer are folded into this single unit of verse and the Christian's evangelistic objective is stated in pictorial terms.

The contrary conjunction *but* has been inserted to convey contrast with the disobedient which are portrayed in 2:7-8. Then Peter begins to link together four pictorial pearls into a beautiful identification bracelet. "You are a chosen people" inflates the self-appraisal of these persecuted peoples. The word for people is *genos* which could be translated *race*. Those who have been responsive to the gospel have been adopted into the family of God. They have been given a new pedigree, a new genealogy. The phrase "chosen people" was applied to Israel in the Old Testament, but now is expanded to include Gentiles who have affirmed their need of salvation. The adjective *ekletos* suggests a uniqueness, a preference. (See chapter 1.) It could be translated, "selecting the best from all choices." Again, these types of labels must have enhanced the esteem of Peter's readers who were physically dislocated because of their faith, but were spiritually grounded in God's amazing grace.

The "priesthood of believers" is one of the most powerful designations in the Bible. This concept served as one of the primary catalysts for the Protestant Reformation. Martin Luther, the leader of the Reformation, emphasized the biblical truth that *every* Christian was a priest before God! Luther penned this comprehensive commentary on the priesthood of believers:

> Therefore all Christians are priests; the men, priests, the women, priestesses, be they young or old, masters or servants, mistresses or maids, learned or unlearned. Here there is no difference, unless faith be unequal.[9]

This inclusive view of the priesthood has been reaffirmed by every generation since the Reformation. Another voice is heard from A.B. Simpson, founder of The Christian and Missionary Alliance, who supports Luther's assessment: "For the priesthood is not confined to any exclusive class as in the Aaronic line, but we are all called to be priests of unto God."[10]

In their academic monograph *Major Bible Themes*, Lewis Sperry Chafer and John F. Walvoord summarize the biblical role of the priesthood and the believer's participation in the ministry:

> Service which God appoints, whether of the Old or New Testament order, is committed primarily to a divinely fitted priesthood. In the Old Testament order the priesthood was a hierarchy over the nation, and in their service they were under the authority of the high priest. In the New Testament order every believer is a priest unto God (1 Peter 2:5-9; Revelation 1:6). The whole ministering company of New Testament priests is under the authority of Christ, who is the true High Priest.[11]

If the contemporary Church could grasp this concept of the all-inclusive priesthood, revival would break out like wildfire in a dry forest. The clergy-driven Church is subject to limited ministry and parochial outreach. If every believer were activated and unleashed for ministry, evangelism would be epidemic, discipleship would exponentially escalate and the Church would be overcrowded with dynamic believers. Too many are spectators who sit in the stands and watch the battle.

One church adopted this vision statement: "Every member growing, ministering, witnessing!" We need less spectators and more players. Bud Wilkerson, who coached Oklahoma University to several national championships, was asked, "What does the game of football do for the health and fitness of America?" His answer is a classic: "I define football as 22 men on the field desperately in need of a rest, and 76,000 people in the stands desperately in need of exercise." The priesthood is for every authentic Christian.

The third description applied to believers is that they comprise "a holy nation." This is drawn from the Old Testament, Exodus 19:6, which is also the first reference to the priesthood of believers. The distinction not only applies to the Jewish nation, but has elasticity in the New Testament to envelop Gentile believers. This nation serves as a counterculture, to display a righteous contrast to the nations around it. The Church, at its best, displays a vivid contrast to the world; at its worst, it cannot be distinguished from the culture in which it exists.

The fourth graphic label is a precious one which communicates God's possessiveness: "a people belonging to God." The King James Version's famous translation is "a peculiar people." Robertson links this translation to the Latin word for *flock* which is *pecus.* [12] This phrase could be translated "a people of God's acquisition." Wycliffe translated the phrase this way: "a people of purchasing." It is inevitable that the believer feels alienated from the culture because of theological and moral differences, and sometimes because of persecution and oppression, but the Christian always "belongs," because God holds him or her in His hand!

Peter concludes 2:9 with the *mission statement* of the believer, "that you may declare the praises of him who called you out of darkness into his wonderful light." Jesus, in one of His "I Am" statements, announced, "I am the light of the world. Whoever follows me will never walk in darkness, but will have the light of life" (John 8:12). He has pierced our darkness and shuttled us into the brightness of the light. However, He has asked every believer to be a light, and the same Greek word is used in Matthew 5:14-16 to present the challenge of illuminating the darkness:

> You are the light of the world. A city on a hill cannot be hidden. Neither do people light a lamp and put it under a bowl. Instead they put it on its stand, and it gives light to

everyone in the house. In the same way, let
your light shine before men, that they may
see your good deeds and praise your Father
in heaven.

One spring in my first church I noticed that the
sanctuary seemed to be darker than before. Upon
inspection, I discovered that *twenty-eight* light
bulbs were out. Each bulb displayed 560 watts of
light. Can you imagine the difference to that worship setting when the light bulbs were shining
again! The follower of Jesus must understand that
one candle can overcome a room full of darkness.

Under the picture of Peter Milne, hanging in
the church he founded on the tiny New Hebrides
Island of Nguana, are found these words: "When
he came there was no light. When he died there
was no darkness."

The apostle utilizes the principle of recur-
rence to reinforce the issue of his audience belonging to God. He extrapolates from the minor
prophet Hosea, "I will plant her for myself in
the land; I will show my love to the one I called
'Not my loved one.' I will say to those called
'Not my people,' 'You are my people'; and they
will say, 'You are our God' " (2:23). The ancient
prophet was referring to disobedient Israel and
God's restoring love which would be granted because of His graciousness. Paul would use this
same verse to illustrate God's love for the Gentiles who were being grafted into the family tree
of the Jewish people.

Peter incorporates this verse in a dual manner, for his readership included both Jew and Gentile. The progression is sequential, first the Jews (Hosea), then the Gentiles (Paul in Romans), then Jew and Gentile (Peter). These Asian Christians were outcasts in their society but they stood in the inner circle of God's family, designed by grace.

The heavenly Father is engaged in building an alliance of peoples to worship and witness in this present world. The book of Revelation accents this "rainbow coalition":

> After this I looked and there before me was a great multitude that no one could count, from every nation, tribe, people and language, standing before the throne and in front of the Lamb. They were wearing white robes and were holding palm branches in their hands. And they cried out in a loud voice:

> "Salvation belongs to our God,
> who sits on the throne,
> and to the Lamb." (Revelation 7:9-10)

Conclusion

The identity of the Christian must not become a foggy gray. There should be a crisp and contrasting distinctiveness which is easily detected in the believer's life. Do you demonstrate a contrast?

Are your family members and friends convinced by your biography that you are an authentic Christian?

During the Vietnam War it was diffcult to distinguish between the North and South Vietnamese. One of my seminary friends revealed the true story of a North Vietnamese soldier who had been submarining under the fences surrounding an American encampment. He had been watching many of the movies which were shown to American soldiers and South Vietnamese allies. It took a long time for him to be discovered because he was not easily distinguished from his former countrymen.

May the world around each and every Christian not encounter the same difficulty. May the contrast be so evident that the disciples of Jesus Christ are clearly marked and identified!

Discussion Questions for Further Study

1. What are some of the word pictures used in the Bible to identify believers and their position and function in Jesus Christ?

2. What are some "spirtual disciplines" for the Christian to include in his or her daily diet?

3. Who are some persons in your circle of influence that you could minister to as a priest for Jesus Christ?

4. Where do you think your light shines most for the kingdom of God?

5. What are some contemporary analogies that might be employed to portray an authentic Christian?

Endnotes

1 This word is used *eight times* in the New Testament in such verses as Acts 7:58 where the witnesses to Stephen's torture and death "laid their clothes" at the feet of Saul [Paul], and in James 1:21 where the reader is challenged to "get rid of all moral filth and the evil that is so prevalent and humbly accept the word planted in you, which can save you."

2 J. Oswald Sanders, *In Pursuit of Maturity* (Grand Rapids, MI: Zondervan, 1986), 15.

3 A.W. Tozer, *The Pursuit of God* (Camp Hill, PA: Christian Publications, 1982), 20.

4 John Milton, *Lycida* (1637), line 123.

5 John Stott, *One People* (Old Tappan, NJ: Revell, 1968), 28-29.

6 *Unger's Bible Dictionary* defines the cornerstone: ". . . the stone at the corner of two walls and uniting them; specifically, the stone built into one corner of the foundation of an edifice as the actual or nominal starting point of a building."—Merrill F. Unger, *Unger's Bible Dictionary*, 3rd ed. (Chicago: Moody, 1966), 223.

7 Lari Goss, "Cornerstone," HeartWarming Music, 1976, 1981.

8 The NIV study notes concisely convey the three options which are fuel for each argument, depending on one's perspective. Some see here an indication that some people are destined to fall and be lost. Others say that unbelievers are destined to be lost because God in His foreknowledge (cf. 1:2) saw them as unbelievers. Still others hold that Peter means that unbelief is destined to

result in eternal destruction.—Kenneth Barker, *The NIV Study Bible* (Grand Rapids, MI: Zondervan, 1985), 1890.

[9]   Martin Luther, *Works of Martin Luther*, 6 vols. (Grand Rapids, MI: Baker, 1982), Vol. 1, 316.

[10] A.B. Simpson, *The Epistles of Peter, John and Jude* (Harrisburg, PA: Christian Publications, n.d.), 38.

[11] Lewis Sperry Chafer and John F. Walvoord, rev. ed., *Major Bible Themes* (Grand Rapids, MI: Zondervan, 1974), 247.

[12] Archibald Thomas Robertson, *Word Pictures in the New Testament*, The General Epistles and the Revelation of John, vol. 6 (Grand Rapid, MI: Baker, 1933), 99.

5

The Imperative of Christian Conduct in a Non-Christian Culture

1 Peter 2:11-25

Dear friends, I urge you, as aliens and strangers in the world, to abstain from sinful desires, which war against your soul. Live such good lives among the pagans that, though they accuse you of doing wrong, they may see your good deeds and glorify God on the day he visits us.

Submit yourselves for the Lord's sake to every authority instituted among men: whether to the king, as the supreme authority, or to governors, who are sent by him to punish those who do wrong and to commend those who do right. For it is God's will that by doing good you should silence the ignorant talk of foolish men. Live as free men, but do not use your freedom as a cover-up for evil; live as servants of God. Show proper

respect to everyone: Love the brotherhood of be-
lievers, fear God, honor the king.

Slaves, submit yourselves to your masters
with all respect, not only to those who are good
and considerate, but also to those who are harsh.
For it is commendable if a man bears up under
the pain of unjust suffering because he is con-
scious of God. But how is it to your credit if you
receive a beating for doing wrong and endure it?
But if you suffer for doing good and you endure
it, this is commendable before God. To this you
were called, because Christ suffered for you,
leaving you an example, that you should follow
in his steps.

> *"He committed no sin,*
> *and no deceit was found in his mouth."*

When they hurled their insults at him, he did
not retaliate; when he suffered, he made no
threats. Instead, he entrusted himself to him who
judges justly. He himself bore our sins in his
body on the tree, so that we might die to sins and
live for righteousness; by his wounds you have
been healed. (1 Peter 2:11-25)

CYRPIAN, BISHOP OF CARTHAGE, WROTE
a letter to his friend Donatus in the third
century which expresses Peter's goal for
the scattered believers of the first century:

It is a bad world, Donatus, an incredibly bad world. But I have discovered in the midst of it a quiet and holy people, who have learned a great secret. They have found a joy which is a thousand times better than any of the pleasures of our sinful life. They are despised and persecuted, but they care not. They are masters of their souls. They have overcome the world. These people, Donatus, are Christians . . . and I am one of them.[1]

Peter's challenge to his readers and, by extension, his challenge to the contemporary Christian was basic: *Conduct yourself as a holy Christian in a hostile non-Christian world!* Live the paradox. Be a counterculture resident of a sin-plagued world. The objective is still relevant for today's disciple: *Be in the world but not of it.* In the first two verses of this section (2:11-12) he issues the generic challenge, which is followed by specific challenges, to pursue Christian conduct in different venues, including government, employment, family and the local church.

Religious Aliens (2:11-12)

Peter initiates this section with an affectionate term: "Dear friends" (2:11). He exhorts them as "aliens and strangers in the world." The word for *alien* appeared in the first verse of his letter to convey the nature of the Christian's residency on the planet earth. The believer is out of step with this world and the citizenship papers list another country, the "commonwealth of heaven," as the home address. An old hymn, "This World Is Not My Home," concisely communicates the status and sensitivities of the authentic Christian:

> This world is not my home,
>   I'm just a passing thru,
> My treasures are laid up
>   somewhere beyond the blue;
> The angels beckon me
>   from heaven's open door,
> And I can't feel at home
>   in this world anymore.
> O Lord, you know
>   I have no friend like you,
> If heaven's not my home
>   then Lord, what will I do?;
> The angels beckon me
>   from heaven's open door,
> And I can't feel at home
>   in this world anymore.

The sad assessment is that many Christians appear to be addicted to the culture rather than allergic to it, especially in the more prosperous nations of the world. Like the Egyptians of old, it appears that some adherents of the Christian faith only hope that the next world is as good as this one! The environment, the ethics and the existential mind-set of this world should have the believer reaching for an inhaler in order to offset the "sinful desires which war against your soul" (2:11)! The apostle makes it crystal clear that the elect should distinguish themselves from the culture in which they live.

The mission is clearly articulated in 2:12: "live . . . good lives" that resonate with "good deeds." Why? Because your accusers will see living proof, a video of your faith, and glorify God. The best promotion for Christianity are those who model it successfully. Barclay wrote:

> Whether we like it or not, every Christian is an advertisement for Christianity; by his life he either commends it to others or makes them think less of it. The strongest missionary force in the world is a Christian life.[2]

Paul characterized Christians as "letters" when he wrote to the church at Corinth:

> You yourselves are our letter, written on our hearts, known and read by everybody. You show that you are a letter from Christ, the result of our ministry, written not with ink but with the Spirit of the living God, not on tablets of stone but on tablets of human hearts. (2 Corinthians 3:2-3)

Each believer should reflect upon the inevitable fact that his or her life will be a classified ad for the Christian faith. The question is not, "Will anyone be affected by my witness?" Rather, the question is, "How many people today will be affected by my witness?" Jesus spoke of this promotional role in the Sermon on the Mount: "In the same way, let your light shine before men, that they may see your good deeds and praise your Father in heaven" (Matthew 5:16).

The disparity between theory and practice is a devastating handicap to modern evangelism. When those who have not accepted Jesus Christ watch the holy life, it is a compelling attraction. The "sermonic life" can harvest many converts. This actual "good life/good deed" illustration highlights the magnetism of such a life:

> The story is told of a university student who wandered into a church one Sunday morning. When the preacher said, "Let us everyone bow his head and pray," the student didn't do that. He had not come to pray. As he looked around he noticed his professor of science who was praying. The student reported, "When I looked upon the face of my professor after the prayer, I saw reflected in there rest, peace and contentment—the very things I had wanted and could not find." Years later the student told his professor, "Thank you for showing the way by your good works, and now as a medical missionary I am doing my best to show others the way."[3]

The Christian does live in a "goldfish bowl" but the "fish" are also watching! Peter understood that reality and so must you and I.

The phrase, "on the day he visits us" (1 Peter 2:12), has been interpreted several ways. Some possibilities include (1) the second coming of Jesus Christ; (2) the judgment day when rewards and retributions are dispersed; or (3) when an unbeliever is converted by the life and ministry of a believer. Regardless, God will be glorified, and the believer can be a component of the equation of exaltation!

Citizens (2:13-17)

What is the Christian response to government? Does conversion alter one's allegiance to the state? Is the Christian subject to civil authorities since Jesus Christ has all authority? At the time of Peter's letter, Jews and Christians were exposed to the power and prestige of the Roman Empire. Instruction was imperative because any action could result in significant repercussions for other Christians and perhaps for the movement itself.

The key word is *submit*. The apostle summons his audience to "Submit yourselves for the Lord's sake to every authority instituted among men" (2:13). He explicitly mentions kings (2:13) and governors (2:14) in this passage. Nevertheless, the command extends far beyond these two positions of power and authority.

The word for *submit*, *hupotasso*, is "primarily a military term" meaning "to rank under."[4] It cre-

ates the context of hierarchy, where one person or
group of people has authority over another person
or group of people. Although the Christians were
"new creations" (2 Corinthians 5:17) and received
spiritual equality in Jesus Christ (Galatians 3:26-
29), this did not abrogate the moral obligation to
existing governmental institutions.

We should not overlook that Paul clearly defined
institutions of government as originating with the
Almighty God. In the Roman letter he asserts:
"Everyone must submit himself to the governing
authorities, for there is no authority except that
which God has established. The authorities that exist have been established by God" (13:1). In a pastoral letter to Timothy, his apprentice, he pleaded
for prayer in respect to civil authorities:

> I urge, then, first of all, that requests,
> prayers, intercession and thanksgiving be
> made for everyone—for kings and all those
> in authority, that we may live peaceful and
> quiet lives in all godliness and holiness. (1
> Timothy 2:1-2)

Paul, as Peter contends in his inspired letter (1 Peter 2:14), endorses submission to government because it works to provide order and peace in
society. The Christian was tutored to be a model
citizen in society. Oswald Sanders capsulized the
objective: "No matter, [Peter] says, what may be
the condition of the community to which you be-
long, behave yourself as a saint in it."[5]

The first readers of Peter's letter and the contemporary students of this same letter wrestle
with the issue of submission, of putting oneself
under the authority of another. There is a spirit of
rebellion and a contempt for authority which fla-
vors today's society. The issue of rights is a domi-
nant one, and the literature and strategies which
accompany different civil causes have chiseled
away at the act of submission. To submit is now
viewed as a weakness, the posture and practice of
a non-achiever, a loser. Richard Foster, however,
in *Celebration of Discipline*, calls our society, especially Christians, back to this biblical lifestyle:

> The Discipline of Submission has been
> terribly misconstrued and abused from fail-
> ure to see the wider context. Submission is
> an ethical theme that runs the gamut of the
> New Testament. It is a posture obligatory
> upon *all* Christians: men as well as women,
> fathers as well as children, masters as well as
> slaves. We are commanded to live a life of
> submission because Jesus lived a life of sub-
> mission, not because we are in a particular
> place or station in life.[6]

In an age which applauds assertiveness and de-
fends civil liberties and rights, this subordination
is rare. The lack of submission has led to civil
wars, church splits and marriage breakdowns.
And who can deny that people do not respect government or the laws which are enforced by gov-

ernmental bodies? The rebirth of this Christian trait would bring radical change and restoration to society.

But there are limits to compliance and submission. Even Peter manifested civil disobedience when he was commanded not to speak or teach in the name of Jesus. His duet with John was curt and courageous: "But Peter and John replied, 'Judge for yourselves whether it is right in God's sight to obey you rather than God. For we cannot help speaking about what we have seen and heard' " (Acts 4:19-20). The tether had reached its end and snapped!

The three Hebrew children, Shadrach, Meshach and Abednego, manifested this same posture before King Nebuchadnezzar (Daniel 3). Despite these and other exceptions, the rule is that Christians support the institutions of government within their nation, state and community.

Peter articulates a simple principle for living, namely, "it is God's will that by doing good you should silence the ignorant talk of foolish men" (1 Peter 2:15). The best way to put out the fires of criticism is to do the right thing, despite pressures and the changing mores that accompany governmental and societal changes. The Christian does not have to fly a trial balloon or take a public opinion poll before he or she acts; rather, the good works which emerge from a life which is Spirit-filled will function like torpedoes which render the guns of enemy ships silent!

If the disciple listens to the critiques of those that are in his or her neighborhood or tries to adjust the fluctuating moralities of different administrations, there will be evident in his or her life a schizophrenic lifestyle. Do the right thing! Do what God has called you to do, and the critic's mouth will be zippered. A.W. Tozer addresses this issue:

> There is a foolish consistency which brings us into bondage to the consciences of other people, but this morality by public pressure is not pure morality at all. At best it is a timid righteousness of doubtful parentage; at worst it is the child of weakness and fear.
>
> A free Christian should act from within with a total disregard for the opinions of others. If a course is right he should take it because it is right, not because he is afraid not to take it. Any act done because we are afraid not to do it is of the same moral quality as the act that is not done because we are afraid to do it.[7]

Stanley Mooneyham reduced his life to a simple principle which parallels the "Peter principle" of 2:15:

> Let what you do arise out of who you are. Being is more important than doing. As for me, I have decided that whatever I do for

the rest of my life, it will not be in order to
have an identity. It will be the result of al-
lowing my God-given self to emerge. I'm
done with posturing for a public that demands an unattainable and hypocritical perfection.[8]

What about the liberties which are guaranteed
by governments?

"Live as free men" (2:16), take advantage of the
benefits which accrue from the order and stability
and peace which governments provide. But the
warning accompanies this circumstance, *don't let
your liberty be translated into license,* into a masquer-
ade for doing evil! Again the message of doing
good is reinforced—good government is an opportunity for the exercise of good works which glorify God. Government becomes a friend to the
servant of God!

In 2:17 Peter recites some of the good works
which he is commending to Christian citizens who
must live under the canopy of earthly administrations. Four goods works are listed in short, stac-
cato pronouncements:

1) "Show proper respect to everyone"
2) "Love the brotherhood of believers"
3) "Fear God"
4) "Honor the king"

It is the final one which in that historical context was the most difficult to obey. The date of

Peter's letter is assigned to the early A.D. '60s A.D. which corresponds to the reign of Nero (A.D.54-68) Nero is one of the most infamous of the Caesars for many reasons. His brutal treatment of those who threatened his throne; the assassination of Vestinus who had married Messalina, a lady the Emperor had been intimate with; his verdict that the Christians were responsible for the fire of Rome (A.D. 64); and his alleged role in the death of Peter and Paul make him one of history's most unpopular figures. Yet Peter insists that the king, even Nero, be honored. Why? The king is to be honored because the Lord is to be feared and obeyed. Submission to Nero is grounded in submission to God! Indeed, this cross must have been one of the largest ones for the readers of Peter's first letter to bear. This radical ethic echoes the words of Jesus in Matthew 5:43-45:

> You have heard that it was said, "Love your neighbor and hate your enemy." But I tell you: Love your enemies and pray for those who persecute you, that you may be sons of your Father in heaven. He causes his sun to rise on the evil and the good, and sends rain on the righteous and the unrighteous.

This type of lifestyle makes the Christian life an exhilarating adventure!

Slaves/Servants (2:18-24)

As we, two millenia further down the historical

road, study the New Testament era, there is a temptation to impose our present culture and mores upon the peoples and times of another context in history. The word *slave* can make a contemporary Christian cringe, but it is estimated that in the first century as many as 60 million slaves existed in the Roman Empire.[9] The lifestyle of some slaves in human history has been a gruesome chronicle of man's inhumanity to man; but for many slaves in the Roman period, life was fairly normal. Slaves were not only assigned custodial tasks but many had professional roles such as "doctors, teachers, musicians, actors, secretaries, stewards."[10]

The normal word for *slave, doulos,* is not utilized in 2:18. A secondary word for *slaves, oiketai,* which comes from the Greek word for *house, oikos,* is employed. Peter is addressing domestic slaves, household servants who were under the authority of a homeowner or landlord. The same word for *submit* which was used in 2:13 reappears in 2:18. The qualifier which Peter adds to the command for submission is that slaves should submit regardless of the disposition or demeanor of the master. Peter makes his instruction an absolute by stating, "not only to those who are good and considerate, but also to those who are harsh" (2:18). The word for *harsh* is *skolios,* which means "curved," "bent," "not straight."[11] The response of the Christian is not pure physics; every action does not deserve an equal and opposite reaction. The Christian paradox finds believers blessing the one who has cursed them and praying for the one who has persecuted them. This type of living turns a spotlight on the darkness.

It may be God's will for a disciple of Jesus Christ to suffer unjustly. Christians are not immune to being treated with disrespect and disgrace. Peter reveals what enables a disciple to receive commendation when life is unfair. The answer: "God consciousness" (see 2:19). Eugene Peterson makes this helpful commentary on a Christian's earthly journey:

> The Christian life is going to God. In going to God Christians travel the same ground that everyone walks on, breathe the same air, drink the same water, shop in the same stores, read the same newspapers, are the citizens of the same government, pay the same prices for groceries and gasoline, fear the same dangers, are subject to the same pressures, get the same distresses, are buried in the same ground. . . . The difference is that each step we walk, each breath we breathe, we know that we are preserved by God, we know we are accompanied by God.[12]

Many slaves were treated with unfairness. Some were Christians, some were not Christians. The key to discovering the authentic Christian was the manifestation of consistent respect despite the inequitable treatment encountered.

Peter adds a twist to this instruction for slaves
by noting that if you rightly deserve the beating
then there is no credit in the suffering. (See 2:20.)
If you receive an F because you miss too many
questions, then there is no merit or commendation
in it. However, suffering when it is not deserved
and yet continuing to submit to authority is very
commendable. It is a gracious act, a Godlike act,
certainly a Christlike act, to suffer unjustly and
project the Spirit of God in those circumstances.

This brand of Christian testimony was personified by the Ten Boom sisters as they served under
the tyranny of the Germans during their incar-
ceration in Ravensbruck Concentration Camp.
Corrie and Betsie were tested by the inhumanity
of the German guards. They were not perfect in
this Christian reflex. Corrie relates this vignette in
her best selling book, *The Hiding Place:*

Fridays—the recurrent humiliation of
medical inspection. The hospital corridor in
which we waited was unheated, and a fall
chill had settled into the walls. Still we were
forbidden even to wrap ourselves in our
arms, but had to maintain our erect, hands-
at-sides position as we filed slowly past a
phalanx of grinning guards. How there
could have been any pleasure in the sight of
these stick-thin legs and hunger-bloated
stomachs I could not imagine. Surely there
is no more wretched sight than the human
body unloved and uncared for. Nor could I

see the reason for the complete undressing; when we finally reached the examining room a doctor looked down each throat, another—a dentist presumably—at our teeth, a third in between each finger. And that was all. We trooped again down the long, cold corridor and picked up our X-marked dresses at the door.

But it was one of those mornings while we were waiting, shivering, in the corridor, that yet another page in the Bible leapt into life for me.

He hung naked on the cross.

I had not known—I had not thought. . . . The paintings, the carved crucifixes showed at least a scrap of cloth. But this, I suddenly knew, was the respect and reverence of the artist. But oh—at the time itself, on that other Friday—there had been no reverence, no more than I saw in the faces around us now.

I leaned toward Betsie, ahead of me in line. Her shoulder blades stood out sharp and thin beneath her blue mottled skin.

"Betsie, they took *His* clothes too."

Ahead of me I heard a little gasp. "Oh, Corrie. And I never thanked Him. . . ."[13]

The supreme standard for Christian suffering is embodied in Jesus Christ. As Blum capsulizes, "Peter's exhortation for Christians to be submissive now receives a Christological foundation."[14]

The example was extrapolated not from fantasy or human history; the example was drawn from the ranks of Deity! The word for example in 2:21 is *hupogrammos.* William Barclay lends his understanding of the ancient world to this pivotal term:

> The word Peter uses for example is *hupogrammos,* a word which comes from the way in which children were taught to write in the ancient world. *Hupogrammos* can mean two things—an *outline* sketch which the learner had to fill in or the *copyhead of copperplate handwriting* in an exercise book which the child had to copy out on the lines below. Jesus gave us the pattern which we have to follow. If we have to suffer insult and injustice and injury, we have only to go through what he has already gone through.[15]

If believers aspire to be copies of the Master Copy, then we must follow in His steps. His footprints lead through sunshine and rain, justice and injustice, acceptance and rejection. His commitment to His Father's will meant that *His personal comfort and safety was secondary to the mission!* The life of Jesus Christ provides an example of adhering to the map even when it included Gethsemane, Calvary and the garden tomb.

This suffering side of the Christian calling is often misunderstood by the prospective convert or new Christian. It is, however, a basic component of New Testament Christianity. Hudson Taylor wrote about this "suffering gap" in the understanding of the Christian's call to follow Jesus:

It is possible to receive salvation through Christ but still have an imperfect appreciation of the nature and responsibilities of our calling.

To what are we called? To do good, to suffer for it, and to take it patiently.

We are called when we so suffer to take it patiently, thankfully, and joyfully because— seen from a right point of view—there is neither ground nor excuse for impatience. On the contrary, there is abundant cause for overflowing thanks and joy.

To make the message intelligible, it must be lived. Be glad that you have the opportunity to make the grace of God intelligible to unbelievers. The greater the persecutions are, the greater the power of your testimony.[16]

The desert, the dungeon, the catacombs and the cross have all served as platforms for God to shout through His suffering instruments to a world in need of His salvation! The victim becomes a vessel through which God communicates His love and plan.

This phrase "in His steps" has become a defining phrase for the disciples of Jesus Christ. Where would Jesus walk? What would Jesus do? If He is the prototype, then it is imperative that each authentic Christian define his or her life by "what would Jesus do?"

In First Peter 2:22-25, Peter quotes directly and refers indirectly to the Suffering Servant passage in Isaiah 53.

Peter features the "shepherd and sheep" analogy but in a fascinating reversal of roles. Normally, the sheep are sacrificed for the profit and gain of the shepherd. Yet, in this New Testament Suffering Servant passage the Shepherd assumes the function of the sheep and is sacrificed on behalf of His flock. The Shepherd becomes a Lamb. Jesus fulfilled His own description of the Good Shepherd in John 10:11: "I am the good shepherd. The good shepherd lays down his life for the sheep."

Peter provides an inspirational view of the substitutionary atonement of the bleeding Shepherd Lamb! John the Baptizer's description of Jesus at Bethany was prophetic and wrapped in redemptive red: "Look, the Lamb of God, who takes away the sin of the world!" (John 1:29). Theodore remarked that it is "a new and strange method of healing; the doctor suffered the cost, and the sick received the healing."[17] The Overseer (1 Peter 2:25) is oppressed, the Bishop is bruised and the straying sheep are rewarded with "green pastures and still waters."

Jesus Christ's journey on earth is permeated with suffering and submission. Even today, in the modern era, the suffering still persists. Reflect on the treatment of Christians by the communists in the country of Cambodia:

> April of 1975 heralded the springtime rebirth of nature in North America. But in Cambodia it was a wintry harbinger of national genocide.
>
> Phnom-Penh, the nation's capital and center of the pro-Western government, was besieged by the Khmer Rouge. Its defenses were crumbling. Foreigners already had been evacuated, including Alliance missionaries forced to leave the largest church and longest-operating mission in the country.
>
> Just days before the Communist tanks punched through the defensive perimeter and clattered down city streets, about 600 Christians crowded into a house church. They all knew it would be their last service for a long time. After singing and praying, they promised each other that those who survived would return and write their names on the wall. Only three names would appear on the wall years later.
>
> The Khmer Rouge regime headed by Pol Pot branded Christians and other believers "Enemy number three of the Revolution." Along with intellectuals and those associated with foreigners or the former government, they were to be killed—often by clubs and shovels, their lives not worth a bullet.[18]

There are still areas of the world where Christians are brutally beaten. There are still unjustified inquisitions and irrational verdicts which are nailed to the lives of Jesus' faithful followers. There are still subtle and serpentine conspiracies to hold Christians back from climbing the promotional ladder or societal conspiracies to stifle the work of God's kingdom so that light cannot penetrate this present darkness. As believers place their shoes in the footprints of Jesus Christ they must be prepared to be a target. It is inevitable that every Christian will suffer—Peter knows that but moves beyond it to the issue of that day—*how* will they suffer?

The willing and patient sufferer strikes a blow against the dark side and renders a verdict for His Commander-in-Chief. When will Jesus' disciples grasp the power of unjust suffering colliding with a confident sufferer who lives as if God is in control, even when the sky is dark and a cross defiantly challenges the survival of His Son or His children?

Conclusion

Charles Sheldon wrote a novel entitled *In His Steps*, the fictional story of a minister named Henry Maxwell who challenged his congregation to live their lives for one year by this guiding principle, "What would Jesus do?" Many who accepted the challenge found their lives revolutionized by this new approach to living. The editor of the local newspaper used his influence to create a vehicle for morality via the printed page. The college president capitalized on his education to improve the city's ethical health and to address the needs of the poor and oppressed. A businessman became a mentor for hundreds of young men who would establish their own companies. Marriages were entered into and engagements broken based upon the principles which emerged in the life of Jesus.

It is the reasonable expectation of Jesus Christ that when His followers come to a fork in the road, a tight ethical corner, a tough moral decision, they will tender the question, "What would my Master do?" Jesus' own words state it boldly, "Follow Me!" A.B. Simpson framed the issue in poetic terms:

What to do we often wonder,
As we seek some watchword true,
Lo, the answer God has given,
What would Jesus do?
When the shafts of fierce temptation,
With their fiery darts pursue,
This will be your heavenly armor,
What would Jesus do?[19]

Discussion Questions for Further Study

1. Why is the designation "stranger" an appropriate one for the follower of Jesus Christ?

2. What are some of the ways in which a Christian encounters hostility in your culture?

3. What are some opportunities that you have to be a "classified ad" for Jesus Christ?

4. What is the general posture of society toward the attitude of submission? Give some examples.

5. What are some concrete ways that a Christian employee can display Jesus Christ to his or her non-Christian employer? How can a Christian employer influence his or her non-Christian employees for Jesus Christ?

Endnotes

1   Joan Winmill Brown, ed., *Day by Day with Billy Graham* (Minneapolis, MN: World Wide Publications, 1976), August 26.

2   William Barclay, *The Letters of James and Peter, The Daily Study Bible Series,* Vol. 14 (Philadelphia: Westminster Press, 1976), 202.

3   Harold L. Fickett, Jr., *Peter's Principles* (Ventura, CA: Regal Books, 1974), 71-72.

4   W.E. Vine, *Expository Dictionary of New Testament Words,* 4 vols. (Grand Rapids, MI: Zondervan, 1952), Vol. 4, 86.

5   Oswald Chambers, *Daily Thoughts for Disciples* (Grand Rapids, MI: Zondervan, 1990), 45.

6   Richard Foster, *Celebration of Discipline,* rev. ed. (San Francisco: Harper, 1988), 117.

7   A.W. Tozer, *Renewed Day by Day, Vol. 1* (Camp Hill, PA: Christian Publications, 1980), November 17.

8   *Men's Devotional Bible* (Grand Rapids, MI: Zondervan, 1993), 1358.

9   Barclay, *The Daily Study Bible,* 210.

10 Ibid.

11 Alan M. Stibbs, *First Peter, The Tyndale New Testament Commentaries,* reprint ed. (Grand Rapids, MI: Eerdmans, 1983), 114.

12 Eugene Peterson, *A Long Obedience in the Same Direction* (Downers Grove, IL: InterVarsity, 1980), 40.

13 Corrie Ten Boom, *The Hiding Place* (Washington Depot, CT: Chosen Books, 1971), 178-179.

14 Leon Morris et. al. *Hebrews-Revelation, The Expositor's Bible Commentary,* Vol. 12, ed. Frank E. Gaebelein (Grand Rapids, MI: Zondervan, 1981), 235.

15 Barclay, *The Daily Study Bible,* 214.

16 Hudson Taylor, quoted in Bruce H. Wilkinson, exec. ed. *Closer Walk New Testament* (Grand Rapids, MI: Zondervan, 1990), 825.

17 Quoted in Stibbs, *First Peter,* 121.

18 Robert Niklaus, "President's Letter: A Premature Death Notice" (Colorado Springs, CO: The Christian and Missionary Alliance), April 5, 1994, p. 1 of enclosure.

19 A.B. Simpson, *Days of Heaven on Earth* (Camp Hill, PA: Christian Publications, 1984), March 29.

6

The Imperative of Christian Conduct in the Family

1 Peter 3:1-7

Wives, in the same way be submissive to your husbands so that, if any of them do not believe the word, they may be won over without words by the behavior of their wives, when they see the purity and reverence of your lives. Your beauty should not come from outward adornment, such as braided hair and the wearing of gold jewelry and fine clothes. Instead, it should be that of your inner self, the unfading beauty of a gentle and quiet spirit, which is of great worth in God's sight. For this is the way the holy women of the past who put their hope in God used to make themselves beautiful. They were submissive to their own husbands, like Sarah, who obeyed Abraham and called him her master. You are

*her daughters if you do what is right and do not
give way to fear.*

*Husbands, in the same way be considerate as
you live with your wives, and treat them with
respect as the weaker partner and as heirs with
you of the gracious gift of life, so that nothing
will hinder your prayers. (1 Peter 3:1-7)*

CHRISTIANITY DID NOT JUST RESOLVE
domestic problems; it also created them.
When only one partner was transformed
by the regenerative powers of the Holy Spirit,
compliance with the command to submit was
much more difficult. Peter begins this exhortation
to wives by establishing *linkage* with the prior section which has provided Jesus Christ as an example. The Lord dealt with unbelievers; indeed, He
died at their hands; but Christians, including
spouses married to unbelievers, are to follow in
His steps of loving the unlovely and trusting that
there is a redemptive thread being woven through
the injustice and pain.

Wives (3:1-6)

What is the strategy for winning non-Christian,
unbelieving husbands? The answer: *holy living!*
The winning method is predicated on behavior
not words. It is perhaps natural for Christian
wives to resort to verbal strategies, but the inspired writer veers in another direction. It is conduct, not conversation which Peter features as the

correct evangelistic approach. In many homes the unregenerate husband assesses the verbal sermonettes of his wife to be a form of nagging. In this crucial lesson for wives, video supercedes verbal. Indeed, for many women this requires the sacrificial submission that can only be delivered by the Spirit! Pious living, not pious preaching, is a key that must be turned if the door of salvation is to be opened for the unsaved husband.

Augustine, one of the great Church fathers, wrote in his *Confessions* about his mother's winsome behavior which led to his father's conversion:

> She tried to win him to you, preaching you to him by her behavior in which you had made her beautiful to her husband, reverently lovable and admirable in his sight. So she tolerated his infidelities and never had a jealous scene with her husband about them. She awaited your mercy upon him. . . .
>
> Finally, toward the end of his earthly life, she won her husband over to you, and now that he was a believer she no longer had to lament the things she had to tolerate when he was not yet a believer.[1]

Harold L. Fickett provides a more contemporary illustration of this behavioral evangelism:

> As a boy I remember a man in prayer meeting saying, "I was an alcoholic. When

I'd come home my wife would badger me and make life so miserable I could hardly wait to get drunk again. But one night she met me with loving arms, sat me in a chair, gave me coffee, and put me to bed without saying a word. She did this every night for two weeks until I couldn't stand it. 'Why don't you nag me instead of loving me?' I cried. She answered, 'I can't because God loves you.' I couldn't take it anymore. I invited Christ into my heart. We now have a Christ-centered home, and God is blessing."[2]

The wife who submits to an authentic Christian lifestyle without argumentation is following the prescription of Peter for marital evangelism!

In 3:2 Peter returns to a theme that he articulated in 2:12 when he asserts that "video" Christianity has a monumental impact on those who do not embrace the faith. In the prior chapter he is addressing Christian "aliens" who are residents in a "foreign" culture. In chapter 3 he is recycling this analogy for the benefit of Christian wives who must reside in a home with a non-Christian husband.

Lifestyle evangelism has an arsenal of weapons in the battle between good and evil, Christ and Satan. One two-barrel shotgun is constructed of one barrel named *purity* and another barrel named *reverence*. When this is aimed at the unbelieving spouse it can have incredible impact. Wives must take inventory of their ammunition! Each wife must *practice the presence of God* so that the husband is exposed to a living edition of Jesus Christ. In the first Corinthian letter, Paul asserted that "the unbelieving husband has been sanctified through his wife" (7:14). A woman's marriage is often her mission field.

In First Peter 3:3-5 Peter assumes the role of a beauty coach as he delivers a hard-hitting segment on outward versus inward beauty. It should be noted that the intense emphasis on inward beauty does not mandate that a woman neglect her exterior appearance. One pastoral writer tendered this common sense insight:

> This passage (1 Peter 3:3-4) isn't badmouthing cosmetics or taking shots at keeping yourself physically attractive, ladies. It's just encouraging you to *keep it in balance.* . . . Like the old saying, "If the house needs painting, *paint it.*"[3]

The New Testament writers were dealing with a culture which had been saturated with Roman influence. Peter cites three aspects of outward adornment in 3:3: braided hair, gold jewelry and fine clothes. There was an obsessive contemporary interest and investment in hair styles:

> The Roman women of the day were addicted to ridiculous extravagance in the adornment of hair. Juvenal (*Satire*, vi) satirizes these customs. He says: "The attendants will vote on the dressing of the hair as

if a question of reputation or of life were at
stake, so great is the trouble she takes in
quest of beauty; with so many tiers does she
load, with so many continuous stories does
she build up on high her head."[4]

Proverbs pre-dates Peter's assessment that outward beauty is insufficient with a very unsophisti-
cated analogy: "Like a gold ring in a pig's snout is
a beautiful woman who shows no discretion"
(Proverbs 11:22).

The primary objective of the Christian woman
should be inward beauty, not outward beauty. It
is constructive to notice that the words *outward
adorning* come from the Greek word *kosmos,* from
which we derive the English word *cosmetics.* This
word, *kosmos,* also translates as the word *world* or
worldly. The point is very sharp in this text. Inward cosmetics take precedence over outward cosmetics. Is that the reality of the Christian woman
who teaches Sunday school or sings in the choir,
who manages the home or administers a business?
Does she expend herself in "dressing up" her
heart?

Adornment according to Peter should be an
inner, "cardiac" variety. The "instead" which
opens 3:4 suggests a strong contrast to that
which precedes it. The foremost beauty aids of
the Christian woman are internal, not external.
Spiritual beauty grows rather than dimishes
with age. This beauty is unfading. The word
which Peter utilizes is a favorite descriptive in

his first letter. *Aphthartos, unfading,* is used in 1:4 referring to the inheritance that can never perish, and is deployed again in 1:23 to describe the Word of God as "imperishable." One writer defines this word as describing "a freedom from decay or theft to which treasures of the external material kind are all exposed."[5]

Peter describes this unfading beauty with two adjectives which work in tandem with submissiveness; namely, a gentle and quiet spirit. Monumental efforts have been made in the twentieth century to escalate the assertive nature of the woman in modern society. However, very little has been done to encourage the submissive side of femininity. Granted, in most cultures and most generations women have been undervalued and underestimated. Nevertheless, this "unfading" beauty is reflected in the quiet ornaments of the heart. One way to gain respect and to impact the modern world is to wear the "cosmetics" of the kingdom of God!

A.W. Tozer, in commenting on this verse, raised the caution flag about outward fashion at the expense of the biblical norm of internal fashion, which God highly values. The modern-day prophet presented this word to women:

Certainly, I am not going to fill the role of a feminine counselor, but I do want to remind you that the Apostle Peter, a great man of God, taught that true adorning is the lasting beauty that is within. Peter said that there is a glowing but hidden being of the heart, more radiant than all the jewels one can buy!

This ties in with the fact that a Christian woman should be very careful about the kind of person she sets up as a model character and example in daily life. It is a sad thing to have our minds occupied with the wrong kind of people!

English history books will not report that Suzannah Wesley was one of the best-dressed women of her day or that she ever received a medal for social activity. But she was the mother of Charles and John Wesley, those princes of Christian song and theology. She taught her own family, and her spiritual life and example have placed her name high in God's hall of fame for all eternity.

So, if you want to take models to follow day by day, please do not take the artificial, globe-trotting females who are intent only upon themselves, their careers and their publicity! God help us all, men and women of whatever marital, social or domestic status, that we may do the will of God and thus win our crown![6]

In 3:5 Peter makes an appeal based on historical precedent. In generic, not particular fashion, he reminds his audience of the methodology that the holy women of the past followed in making themselves beautiful. This submissive, gentle and quiet spirit had aesthetic value in enhancing the female ancestors of Peter's day and, by extension, the modern woman.

Sarah is featured in 3:6 as the personification of the beautiful woman. Her submissive internal spirit, her willingness to function as the vice-president of Abraham's house, her obedience to the biblical family structure made her an example of womanhood for succeeding generations. Charles Swindoll posed this penetrating question to wives, "Do I love my husband enough to *live* for him?"[7] Sarah understood her role as a Jewish woman and as a covenant woman. Her partnership with Abraham permitted their marriage to endure, their home to be blessed with God's favor and their nation to achieve new dimensions of prosperity!

It is crucial to remember that Jesus Christ was a servant who submitted to His Father's will. To submit is to be Christlike! If there is not submission in a marriage, then tension, not tenderness, prevails. Both parties have been called to submit to each other (Ephesians 5:21). There is reciprocity in the marital dynamics of living and serving each other. But the thrust of this passage is directed toward a Christian wife who is united to a non-Christian husband. The winsome walk, not the talk, will often lead to the conversion of the lost husband. Albert Barnes provides a final exhortation to women who must minister in this "mixed" marital environment:

It is not by a harsh, fretful, complaining temper; it is by kindness, tenderness, and love. It is by demonstrating the excellency of religion; by patience when provoked, meekness when injured, love when despised, forbearance when words of harshness and irritation are used; by kind and affectionate conversation when alone, when the heart is tender, when calamities visit the family. . . .

We are never to cease setting a Christian example; never to cease living as a Christian should live; never to cease praying fervently to the God of grace, that the partner of our lives may be brought under the full influence of Christian truth, and so may enjoy heaven with us.[8]

This path was walked by Jesus Christ as He sought to influence and win His Bride, the Church. It is a difficult path, a journey with many obstacles and many opportunities to display the Spirit-filled life! The footprints have been etched in human history; they are His steps, and the holy woman is called to place her feet in their tracings and her faith in their Maker.

Husbands (3:7)

Peter brings reciprocity and balance to the issue of marital dynamics. The husband is now addressed regarding his obligations to his wife. The woman that he lives with is to receive consideration and respect. In the context of the first century, women were viewed as less valuable to society than men. The woman was a piece of property, an item of furniture.

Skeuos, the word used here, is as Robertson comments, "an old and common word for vessel, furniture, utensil (Matt. 12:29; II Tim. 2:20)."[9] *Both* husband and wife are categorized by this term. The degree of strength or weakness is probably referring to sheer physical strength. A man is superior, in most marriages, in his ability to lift more and run faster. However, it should be noted that in reference to biological strength, the woman is much more resistant to disease and lives longer. The husband should treat the wife as fine china not plastic ware in the realm of physical tasks. She should not be asked to compromise her health and welfare to accomplish physical feats which are more designed for his build and constitution.

The husband is informed that his wife is an heir with him "of the gracious gift of life." This joint-heir designation is another indication of equivalency in the saving benefits of the faith. Paul confirmed this in Galatians 3:28: "There is neither Jew nor Greek, slave nor free, male nor female, for you are all one in Christ Jesus." Elisabeth Elliot commented on this idea of being joint-heirs by asserting that "there is no more beautiful expression in the Bible to describe a married couple."[10] Stuart Briscoe highlights the "stun quality" of this analogy:

This revolutionary teaching by Peter—that women were *equally* heirs of the grace of life—amazed the men of that time. For in Peter and Paul's day, men were the legal heirs of life. They strutted around and had everything going their way. The women entertained them, met their sexual needs, managed their homes and produced their sons (and heirs). Women were locked into roles determined by men.[11]

This verse details the counterculture ethics of the kingdom of God. For the men of the first century the call had been sounded for living the paradox! Husbands who displayed consideration for their wives' needs, who demonstrated a preference for their wives, who counted their wives equivalent in spiritual matters presented a stunning contrast to the prevailing dynamics of marriages in that era.

The husband who did not follow this pattern jeopardized his prayer life! Peter warned them to live in this manner "so that nothing will hinder your prayers" (3:7). A man's power in prayer can be downsized by improper treatment of his wife. His vertical relationship with God is not independent of his horizontal dealings with his wife. There is linkage between the discipline of prayer and the home life of a man. A.W. Tozer takes on this nexus:

I suppose there are many Christian husbands whose prayers are not being answered and they can think up a lot of reasons. But the fact is that thoughtless husbands are simply big, overbearing clods when it comes to consideration of their wives.

If the husband would get himself straightened out in his own mind and spirit and live with his wife according to knowledge, and treat her with chivalry that belongs to her as the weaker vessel, remembering that she is actually his sister in Christ, his prayers would be answered in spite of the devil and all of the other reasons that he gives.

A husband's spiritual problems do not lie in the Kremlin nor in the Vatican but in the heart of man himself—in his attitude and inability to resist the temptation to grumble and growl and dominate!

There is no place for that kind of male leadership in any Christian home. What the Bible calls for is proper and kindly recognition of the true relationships of understanding and love, and the acceptance of a spirit of cooperation between husband and wife.[12]

The husband must move beyond societal and cultural norms; he must follow a more noble and holy ethic, in the name and power of Jesus Christ. In pursuing this nonnegotiable of his faith, he honors His God, honors his wife and honors the next generation by mentoring them in the principle of consideration. Also, he enhances his prayer life, for as Bigg remarks: "The sighs of an injured wife come between a husband's prayers and God's hearing."[13]

Conclusion

The deeper Christian life is imperative for healthy and holy dynamics to be operating in the family. The analogy of a wheel with a hub and many spokes is helpful. If we designate God as the center or hub of the wheel and the spokes as representing individuals, it is a principle of the design that as you move closer to the hub the spokes become closer together. Likewise, the closer one moves to God, the closer one can move to others. Proximity to God enhances the possibility of closer intimacy with others. In marriage, the more intimate a person is with God, the more potential for intimacy with his or her spouse. As the distance increases from God, the potential for improved relationships in marriage diminishes.

If it is true that "one hundred pianos tuned to the same fork are automatically tuned to each other,"[14] then could it not be illustrative that if individuals are tuned to Jesus Christ these persons would be tuned to each other? Those who aspire to have "heaven on earth" in their marriages must pursue God and allow Him to develop their hearts to be holy. A Spirit-filled heart is the best antidote to an anemic marriage.

Discussion Questions for Further Study

1. How does Ephesians 5:21-22 add to the discussion on submitting in marriage relationships?

2. What aspects of modern society make submission more difficult between husband and wife?

3. How does the deeper life contribute to the attitudes on submission?

4. When and how did Jesus Christ submit to anyone or any institution?

5. What are some ways a husband can demonstrate consideration for his wife?

Endnotes

1 Augustine, *Confessions*, trans. Mary Clark, *Augustine of Hippo: Selected Writings* (New York: Paulist Press, 1984), 9, 112-113.

2 Harold L. Fickett, Jr., *Peter's Principles* (Ventura, CA: Regal Books, 1992), 84-85.

3 Charles Swindoll, *Strike the Original Match* (Portland, OR: Multnomah Press, 1980), 46.

4 M.R. Vincent, *Word Studies in the New Testament*, 2 vols. (MacDill AFB, FL: MacDonald Publishing, 1986), 1:309.

5 Alan M. Stibbs, *The Tyndale New Testament Commentaries, First Peter*, reprint ed. (Grand Rapids, MI: Eerdmans, 1983), 125.

6 A.W. Tozer, *Renewed Day by Day, Vol. 1* (Camp Hill, PA: Christian Publications, 1980), September 22.

7 Swindoll, *Strike the Original Match*, 42.

8 Albert Barnes, quoted in Bruce H. Wilkinson, exec. ed., *Closer Walk* (Grand Rapids, MI: Zondervan, 1992), 207.

9 Archibald Thomas Robertson, *Word Pictures in the New Testament, The General Epistles and the Revelation of John*, Vol. 6 (Grand Rapids, MI: Baker, 1933), 110.

[10] Elisabeth Elliot, *Let Me Be a Woman* (Wheaton, IL: Tyndale, 1988), 129.

[11] *Men's Devotional Bible* (Grand Rapids, MI: Zondervan, 1993), 1359.

[12] A.W. Tozer, *Renewed Day by Day*, *Vol. 1*, April 27.

[13] C.S. Bigg quoted in William Barclay, *The Letters of James and Peter*, *The Daily Study Bible Series*, Vol. 14 (Philadelphia: Westminister Press, 1976), 224.

[14] A.W. Tozer, *The Pursuit of God* (Camp Hill, PA: Christian Publications, 1982), 96.

7

The Imperative of Christian Conduct Despite Suffering

1 Peter 3:8-22

Finally, all of you, live in harmony with one another; be sympathetic, love as brothers, be compassionate and humble. Do not repay evil with evil or insult with insult, but with blessing, because to this you were called so that you may inherit a blessing. For,

"Whoever would love life
* and see good days*
must keep his tongue from evil
* and his lips from deceitful speech.*
He must turn from evil and do good;
* he must seek peace and pursue it.*
For the eyes of the Lord are on the righteous
* and his ears are attentive to their prayer,*

but the face of the Lord is against those
        who do evil."

*Who is going to harm you if you are eager to
do good? But even if you should suffer for what
is right, you are blessed. "Do not fear what they
fear; do not be frightened." But in your hearts
set apart Christ as Lord. Always be prepared to
give an answer to everyone who asks you to give
the reason for the hope that you have. But do this
with gentleness and respect, keeping a clear conscience, so that those who speak maliciously
against your good behavior in Christ may be
ashamed of their slander. It is better, if it is
God's will, to suffer for doing good than for doing evil. For Christ died for sins once for all, the
righteous for the unrighteous, to bring you to
God. He was put to death in the body but made
alive by the Spirit, through whom also he went
and preached to the spirits in prison who disobeyed long ago when God waited patiently in
the days of Noah while the ark was being built.
In it only a few people, eight in all, were saved
through water, and this water symbolizes baptism that now saves you also—not the removal
of dirt from the body but the pledge of a good
conscience toward God. It saves you by the resurrection of Jesus Christ, who has gone into heaven
and is at God's right hand—with angels,
authorities and powers in submission to him. (1
Peter 3:8-22)*

N HIS BOOK, *AN EYE FOR AN EYE*, Christopher
J.H. Wright reminds the reader of God's purpose for the covenant community:

> His desire is for a holy people for his own
> possession, a redeemed community, a model
> society through whom he can display a pro-
> totype of the new humanity of his ultimate
> redemptive purpose.[1]

The apostle Peter has some high expectations for
the Church as he begins a summary section which
zeroes in on the dynamics of the Christian in society, in the home and in the Church. The reader is
made aware of his intention to summarize by the
word *finally*.[2] Peter's words are meant for everyone;
there are no exemptions or exclusions to his directives. He lists *five virtues* which, if exercised by
God's people, will create a *community* of Christians
which manifests an attractive antithesis to the world
at large. Unfortunately the Church has experienced
its seasons of discontent and divisions. Those who
have entered a church for a worship event have
sometimes found a war zone.

I read the story of a pastor who was leading
young children in a church spelling bee. He
turned to one child and stated, "Your word today
is *worship.*"

"Warship. W-A-R-S-H-I-P. Warship. Am I
right?" the child asked.

With a deep sigh, the pastor replied, "Yes, unfortunately, much of the time you are!"[3] This is

dysfunctional Christianity which does not honor God nor facilitate the winning of lost men and women. The five virtues of this Scripture must be be present or the attitude of this folksy poem will become reality:

> To dwell above with saints we love,
> O that will be glory;
> To dwell below with saints we know,
> Well, that's another story.
> —Anonymous

Doing Good (3:8-13)

These five virtues form the social agenda for the believer in respect to others within the family of God.

The first societal principle is *to live in harmony with one another* (3:8). There is a likemindedness that is common to the children of God. There should be a common set of core values which govern Christian mission and ministry. There should be a common vision which act to coalesce and bring cohesion to the body of Christ. If everyone goes his or her own way there is chaos and eventually anarchy. The family of God must agree to sing the same song, albeit in different parts. There should be no compromise on essentials, but there should be tolerance on nonessentials.

The second societal principle is *to be sympathetic* (3:8). The original word, *sumpatheis*, means to "feel together," to "share pathos." Paul appealed to this type of lifestyle in Romans 12:15, when he wrote, "Rejoice with those who rejoice; mourn with those who mourn." A church leader many years ago turned my head toward truth when he observed that it is easier to mourn with those that are suffering than it is to rejoice with those that are successful. It is imperative to shed tears of sadness for those in sorrow, but it is *just as holy* to shed tears of gladness for the believer who has achieved great awards!

The apostle Paul, in his first letter to the church at Corinth, framed this idea within the idea of "body life": "If one part suffers, every part suffers with it; if one part is honored, every part rejoices with it" (1 Corinthians 12:26).

The third ethical principle that Peter details is *love as brothers* (3:8). This is obviously the right thing to do, but too often it is not detectable among Christ's body.

According to Jesus Christ, love is the badge of discipleship; and He was not referring to love for God, but rather the love which is expressed toward the human family of God. Tucked into that passionate farewell recorded in the fourth Gospel, our Lord provided the stipulation for our kingdom badge: "By this all men will know that you are my disciples, if you love one another" (John 13:35).

The word in First Peter 3:8 is *philadelphoi*, which is a compound word combining *adelphos (brother)* and one of the words for love, *philos.* Our level of love for each other in God's family should not be underrated! Where love is lacking, evangel-

ism is severely handicapped. The ethics of the
kingdom demand that love be the defining personality trait of the covenant community.

Two other principles are linked in 3:8. *Compassion* and *humility* are paired as obligatory traits of
the genuine disciple. The first word has the thrust
of soft-heartedness and is a relative of sympathy.
The second word refers to a mind that is willing
to consider others' needs and desires above itself.
The word *tapeinophrosune* might be translated *low-
mindedness*.[4]

This mind-set is addressed in several Scripture
verses, including the following:

> Be completely humble and gentle; be pa-
> tient, bearing with one another in love.
> (Ephesians 4:2)

> Do nothing out of selfish ambition or vain
> conceit, but in humility consider others bet-
> ter than yourselves. (Philippians 2:3)

> Therefore, as God's chosen people, holy and
> dearly loved, clothe yourselves with com-
> passion, kindness, humility, gentleness and
> patience. (Colossians 3:12)

It does not require a nuclear physicist to understand that if these five virtues are operating in the
life and work of the Church, it is inevitable that
peace and grace are going to be trademarks of that
body.

William Barclay in his comments on this very passage made a powerful and uncompromising assessment of the Church. In a very frank statement, the Scottish theologian wrote:

All through the New Testament there rings this plea for Christian unity. It is more than a plea; it is an announcement that no man can live the Christian life unless in his personal relationships he is at unity with his fellow men; and that the Church cannot be truly Christian if there are divisions within it.[5]

The famous Pogo cartoon is applicable—the character announces, "We have met the enemy and he is us!" If the Church will practice these five virtues, that possibility will cease to exist!

Meeting Insult with Blessing

In 3:9 the Christian is confronted with a challenge. Evil is not to be met with evil and insult is not to be met with insult; rather, actions of evil and insults are to be met with a *blessing*. Peter includes this as a nonnegotiable for the lifestyle of the redeemed: "to this you were called." In the Old Testament the principle of *lex talionis* (the law of retaliation), "an eye for an eye and a tooth for a tooth," was the *modus operandi*. Actually, this stifled injustice and excessive vengeance because it prevented the victim from taking more than his rightful justice—for example, two eyes and two ears for the loss of one eye. *Lex talionis* was a merciful ethic of the Old Testament period! The standard is upgraded in the New Testament with a principle that does not seek equalization. Rather, the authentic disciple meets his oppressor with grace and love.

The teachings of Jesus in the Sermon on the Mount clearly frame this ethical principle. Matthew 5:38-45 declares:

> You have heard that it was said, "Eye for eye, and tooth for tooth." But I tell you, Do not resist an evil person. If someone strikes you on the right cheek, turn to him the other also. And if someone wants to sue you and take your tunic, let him have your cloak as well. If someone forces you to go one mile, go with him two miles. Give to the one who asks you, and do not turn away from the one who wants to borrow from you.
>
> You have heard that it was said, "Love your neighbor and hate your enemy." But I tell you: Love your enemies and pray for those who persecute you, that you may be sons of your Father in heaven. He causes his sun to rise on the evil and the good, and sends rain on the righteous and the unrighteous."

This passage eliminates the phrase "getting even" from the Christian's vocabulary. Nevertheless, the equalizer mentality is still very much alive in virtually every Christian community. This holy calling summons each believer to rise above the "eye for an eye" principle. David Augsburger, in his small but potent book *The Freedom of Forgiveness,* inserts an old saying which has contemporary merit: "Doing an injury puts you below your enemy; revenging an injury makes you but even with him; forgiving it sets you above him!"[6]

The word *blessing* in 3:9 is *eulogountes* (see 1 Peter 1:3), which is related to the English word *eulogy,* referring to good and benevolent words which are spoken at a funeral. The Christian is assigned the homework of finding a good response to a negative deed. The same word *eulogountes* is found in Stephen's response to those who were making him the first martyr of the early Church. His reaction is reported in Acts 7:60: "Then he fell on his knees and cried out, 'Lord, do not hold this sin against them.' When he had said this, he fell asleep." This personifies the principle which Peter was commending to those first-century adherents of Christianity.

The apostle Paul adds further endorsement of this kingdom ethic in Romans 12:17-21:

> Do not repay anyone evil for evil. Be careful to do what is right in the eyes of everybody. If it is possible, as far as it depends on you, live at peace with everyone. Do not take revenge, my friends, but leave room for God's wrath, for it is written: "It is mine to

avenge; I will repay," says the Lord. On the
contrary:

> "If your enemy is hungry, feed him;
>   if he is thirsty, give him something to
>   drink.
> In doing this, you will heap burning coals
>   on his head."

> Do not be overcome by evil, but overcome
>   evil with good.

Corrie Ten Boom was speaking in Munich,
Germany in 1947 when she recognized one of the
guards that had administered inhumane treatment
to her and her sister Betsie in the Ravensbruck
prison. Her account demonstrates the throbbing
tension that accompanies a personal encounter
with one who has wronged a believer to the point
of sorrowful agony.

> Now he was in front of me, hand thrust
> out: "A fine message, Fraulein! How good it
> is to know that, as you say, all our sins are at
> the bottom of the sea!"
> And I, who had spoken so glibly of for-
> giveness, fumbled in my pocketbook rather
> than take that hand. He would not remem-
> ber me, of course—how could he remember
> one prisoner among those thousands of
> women?
> But I remembered him and the leather

crop swinging from his belt. I was face to face with one of my captors and my blood seemed to freeze.

"You mentioned Ravensbruck in your talk," he was saying. "I was a guard there." No, he did not remember me.

"But since that time," he went on, "I have become a Christian. I know that God has forgiven me for the cruel things I did there, but I would like to hear it from your lips as well. Fraulein,"—again the hand came out— "will you forgive me?"

And I stood there—I whose sins had again and again to be forgiven—and could not forgive. Betsie had died in that place—could he erase her slow terrible death simply for the asking?

It could not have been many seconds that he stood there—hand held out—but to me it seemed hours as I wrestled with the most difficult thing I ever had to do.

For I had to do it—I knew that. The message that God forgives has a prior condition: that we forgive those who have injured us. "If you do not forgive men their trespasses," Jesus says, "neither will your Father in heaven forgive your trespasses."

I knew it not only as a commandment of God but as a daily experience. Since the end of the war I had had a home in Holland for victims of Nazi brutality. Those who were able to forgive their former enemies were able also to return to the outside world and rebuild their lives, no matter what the physical scars. Those who nursed their bitterness remained invalids. It was as simple and as horrible as that. . . .

And so, woodenly, mechanically, I thrust my hand into the one stretched out to me. And as I did an incredible thing took place. The current started in my shoulder, raced down my arm, sprang into our joined hands. And then this healing warmth seemed to flood my whole being, bringing tears to my eyes.

"I forgive you, brother!" I cried. "With all my heart."

For a long moment we grasped each other's hands, the former guard and the former prisoner. I had never known God's love so intensely as I did then.[7]

Corrie Ten Boom verified the product! And so did the first-century group of Christian converts who were scattered over the terrain of the Roman Empire. Perhaps the strongest validation of the Christian faith is love expressed in the face of hate, grace expressed in the presence of inhumanity and forgiveness expressed in the context of unjustified cruelty. The counterculture shouts loudly when a human heart spends good for evil, just as the heavenly Father did when He spent His Son:

But God demonstrates his own love for us in this: While we were still sinners, Christ died for us (Romans 5:8).

The Powerful Tongue

Peter inserts a quote from Psalm 34:12-16, the writing of David, into his letter. The number of people who love living and aspire to good days would be astronomical, virtually inclusive. However, the contingency faces an extremely difficult challenge: namely, to "keep [their] tongue from evil and [their] lips from deceitful speech." The wisdom literature of the Old Testament has tons to say about the mighty muscle, the *tongue*. Its dimensions are small, its potential is enormous. Proverbs features many verses which explicitly detail its potential for building up and breaking down the lives of others (emphasis added):

The *tongue* that brings healing is a tree of life, but a deceitful *tongue* crushes the spirit. (15:4)

The *tongue* has the power of life and death, and those who love it will eat its fruit. (18:21)

The book of James has a lengthy discourse on the tongue which provides three analogies of its astounding influence. First, it is compared to a *bit* in a horse's mouth (3:3). A one-pound bit can manipulate a one-thousand-pound thoroughbred. Secondly, it is analogous to the *rudder* of a ship (3:4-5) which is extremely insignificant when compared to the vital statistics of a ship, but which weighs heavily on the direction the ship will sail. Thirdly, the tongue is equated to a *spark* (3:5-6) which can obliterate an entire forest which has been created over hundreds of years.

The Christian should not underestimate the value of what he or she speaks, for words can build or bludgeon relationships. David issued this prayer which is appropriate for any generation: "Set a guard over my mouth, O LORD; keep watch over the door of my lips" (Psalm 141:3).

First Peter 3:11 highlights a crucial Christian principle. It is not enough to refrain from evil; "He must turn from evil." But it is also imperative that we be proactive in administering holy deeds: "do good." One of my pastors made the remark, "People know more of what we are against than what we are for!"

Edmund Burke made this cutting assessment: "The only thing necessary for the triumph of evil is for good men to do nothing."[8]

Peter advocates a proactive pursuit of peace which falls under the canopy of a man's pursuit of God. The pursuit dovetails with the five virtues which are cataloged in 3:8. Jesus linked those who pursue peace with the status of being a child of the heavenly Father: "Blessed are the *peacemakers*, for they will be called sons of God" (Matthew 5:9, emphasis added). The apostle Paul hitchhiked with this theme throughout his letters. Three references supply ample evidence that he was aboard the "Peace Train" (emphasis added):

> If it is possible, as far as it depends on you, live at *peace* with everyone. (Romans 12:18)

> Let us therefore make every effort to do what leads to *peace* and to mutual edification. (Romans 14:19)

> Finally, brothers, good-by. Aim for perfection, listen to my appeal, be of one mind, live in *peace*. And the God of love and *peace* will be with you. (2 Corinthians 13:11)

In his book *Healing the Dysfunctional Church Family*, David Mains included this short but strategic prayer:

> Father,
> I know that no church is perfect,
> So help me not to be surprised when
>   problems arise.
> Keep me from pointing a finger of blame
>   at others;
> Guard my tongue from shameful remarks.
> Grant me the courage to do my part to make
>   our church a better place.
> And thank you for graciously allowing me to
>   be part of the best family in the
>   world. Amen.[9]

First Peter 3:12 delineates the demarcation of the divine Judge. There have always been *two* ways (cf. Matthew 7:13-14). Once the road is chosen, you cannot choose the destination.

The watershed of the United States is called the Continental Divide. The water that flows down one side ends up in the Atlantic Ocean, the water that flows down the other side ends up in the Pacific Ocean. Whichever side the water flows determines its oceanic destination. Likewise, in the lives of humanity, the choice of sides is deterministic. The righteous have the eyes and ears of the Lord fixed on them, and prayers are answered. But those who do evil will stare into the face of the Lord.

Psalm 1 is one of the most effective pieces of biblical literature in portraying the theological divide between saints and sinners, between the people of God and the people who oppose God. It functions as one of the most promising texts for believers and serves as one of the most punishing texts for unbelievers. *There is no neutral ground,* no demilitarized zone. Listen to its description of the two lifestyles which are available for every man and woman:

> Blessed is the man
>   who does not walk in the counsel of the
>   wicked
> or stand in the way of sinners
>   or sit in the seat of mockers.
> But his delight is in the law of the LORD,

and on his law he meditates day and
    night.
He is like a tree planted by streams of water,
    which yields its fruit in season
and whose leaf does not wither.
    Whatever he does prospers.

Not so the wicked!
    They are like chaff
    that the wind blows away.
Therefore the wicked will not stand in the
        judgment,
    nor sinners in the assembly of the righ-
        teous.

For the LORD watches over the way of the
        righteous,
    but the way of the wicked will perish.

"Who is going to harm you if you are eager to
do good?" (3:13). God is in control, and though, as
Peter relates in the next section, you may suffer
penultimate harm, ultimately God will honor His
Word and His people! "Do-gooders" obey Him
and are truly the kingdom builders in this world!

Suffering for the Right (3:14-22)

Peter is writing to Christians who are being
singed by the flames of persecution. Fairness and
equity were not guaranteed for the first-century
Christian. The playing field was not level! He returns to the theme of suffering and, in particular,

to the theme of *suffering unjustly* (cf. 2:20-22). The Greek construction in 3:14 features a "not probable but possible" thrust. But Peter's references and history's record reveals that these believers were passing through the gauntlet.

Isaiah 8:12-13 is the foundation for the latter part of 3:14. The background is rather dismal. King Ahaz of Judah has opted to forge an alliance with the dreaded Assyrians. Israel and Syria are now threatening to invade his territory. Ahaz is showing symptoms of panic.

Isaiah's words remind him that he should not fear human kings or armies, but his fear should be in response to Yahweh, the Lord Almighty. In other words, don't fear what men will do to you; trust in God, and fear only Him! The application is clear: When men and women inflict the Christian with the needle of suffering, he or she is to understand that God is still in control. Jesus spoke to this issue in the Beatitudes:

> Blessed are those who are persecuted
>   because of righteousness,
>   for theirs is the kingdom of heaven.

> Blessed are you when people insult you, persecute you and falsely say all kinds of evil against you because of me. Rejoice and be glad, because great is your reward in heaven, for in the same way they persecuted the prophets who were before you. (Matthew 5:10-12)

Undeserved hardships, harrasssments and hurts can be tools which God deploys to fashion *conformity to Jesus Christ*.

The early Christians are reported to have rejoiced that they were worthy to suffer for the person and work of Jesus Christ. In Romans 8:18, Paul evaluates his pain in these terms: "I consider that our present sufferings are not worth comparing with the glory that will be revealed in us." The Christian is asked to take the "long view" of suffering. The road sign reads: "Temporary inconvenience, permanent improvement."

Acts 5:41 is another example of this long, wide-angle view of suffering: "The apostles left the Sanhedrin, rejoicing because they had been counted worthy of *suffering* disgrace for the Name" (emphasis added). In his book, *Where Is God When It Hurts?*, Philip Yancey offers an excellent illustration on the eternal perspective:

How to imagine eternity? It's so much larger than our short life here that it's hard to visualize. You can go to a ten-foot blackboard and draw a line from one side to another. Then, make a one-inch dot in that line. To a microscopic germ cell, sitting in the midst of that one-inch dot, it would look enormous. The cell could spend its lifetime exploring its length and breadth. But, you're not a cell, you're a human, and by stepping back to view the whole blackboard you're suddenly struck with how *huge* that ten-foot line is compared to the tiny dot that germ cell calls home.

It's the same way with eternity compared to this life. Seventy years is a long time, and we can develop a lot of ideas about God and how indifferent He appears to suffering in seventy years. But is it reasonable to judge God and His plan for the universe by the swatch of time we spend on earth? No more reasonable than for that germ cell to judge a whole blackboard by the tiny smudge of chalk where he spends his life. Is that a just trail? Have we missed the perspective of the universe and of timelessness?[10]

Set Apart the Interior

The Christian majors on the interior. Peter reinforces this thesis with his command in 3:15: "But in your hearts *set apart* Christ as Lord" (emphasis added). The heart is symbolic of the worship center of man. The inner sanctuary of our existence is to be reserved seating for Jesus Christ. The word for *set apart* is a form of the word *hagiazo*, which is the verb for "to make holy."

The act of creating honored space for Jesus Christ is a sacred one. Robert Munger wrote a small booklet in 1954 which he titled, "My Heart, Christ's Home." It has been reprinted more than forty times. It is an effective tool in visualizing our heart as a home with many rooms. As Munger unwraps his analogy he invites Christ to dwell in every room of his heart. His closing words ring loudly with the theme of lordship. He concludes:

> Dropping to my knees, I said, "Lord, You have been a guest and I have been the host. From now on I am going to be the servant. You are going to be the Lord." Running as fast as I could to the strongbox, I took out the title deed to the house describing its properties, assets, and liabilities. I eagerly signed the house over to Him alone for time and eternity. "Here," I said, "Here it is, all that I am and have, forever. Now you run the house. I'll just remain with you as servant and friend."
>
> Things are different since Jesus Christ has settled down and has made His home in my heart.[11]

Be an Apologist

Apologetics is the defense of the standards of the Christian's faith and life. Peter asserts that every believer is encompassed by this branch of theology: "Always be prepared to give an answer (*apologian*) to everyone who asks you to give the reason for the hope that you have" (3:15). Every disciple should be able to articulate the rationale for his or her beliefs. There should be no hesitation, no delay, no stutter. The Christian faith is defensible! It might be assumed that Peter is speaking of public interrogation by civil or church officials. However, the context and the Greek words chosen by Peter point to a more generic audience and task. The original word for *asks* is *aitein*, which refers to ordinary conversation, not official language.

Effective discipleship prepares every man and woman who follows Jesus Christ to be capable of explaining the rationale for their commitment to His Lordship. If we asked a person why he or she chose to live in a certain community, to be educated in a certain college or to marry a particular person, we would expect an immediate and logical answer. Even more critical is the response when someone poses the question, "Why are you a Christian?" This answer for the Christian hope should not be draped in condescension or arrogance, but Peter counsels that it should be clothed with gentleness and respect (3:15).

In 3:16, the great apostle links the "clear conscience" to effective witnessing. The verse broaches again the issue of those who slander and speak maliciously of good behavior. The conscience functions as a "traffic light" signaling whether there is a green light, yellow light or red light situation. Oswald Chambers contributes enlightening comment on this element of Christian living:

> Conscience is that faculty in me which attaches itself to the highest I know, and tells me what the highest I know demands I do.

It is the eye of the soul which looks out either toward God or toward what it regards as the highest authority.[12]

Suffering for Holy Causes

The suffering of the Christian is broached again in 3:17. Suffering for holy and righteous causes can be within the sphere of God's will. Joseph was permitted to suffer in a plurality of ways, but every adversity was orchestrated by the Lord so that one day he would earn Pharaoh's favor and exercise the influence which would save the Hebrew people during the seven year famine.

Job was a righteous man and his suffering approached incredible proportions, but he was resilient and maintained his faith in a sovereign and just God. And Jesus Christ fashioned the articles of man's atonement through the instrumentality of a cross. Joseph, Job and Jesus Christ passed through the fire of suffering and emerged purer than gold.

Persecution can demonstrate the power of God! One of the ancient heroes of the faith bears testimony to what God can enable a believer to do in the midst of unfair, illegitimate and unwarranted suffering. Polycarp was in his eighties when he was commanded to disavow his loyalty to Jesus Christ. If he did not, he would be burned at the stake.

He did not recant, and the fire still burns in the

hearts of Christendom from the kindling of Polycarp's sacrifice. He was martyred at Smyrna in A.D. 156, but his afterglow is seen around the world and through the ages!

The "suffering for good" thesis that Peter shuttles to the surface in 3:17 is personified by Jesus Christ in 3:18: "Christ died for sins once for all, the righteous for the unrighteous." This is the redeeming paradox: *He took what we deserved that we might receive what He deserved*. Many Bible passages explicitly detail this substitutionary atonement. One of the most prominent appears in the writings of Isaiah:

> But he was pierced for our transgressions,
>   he was crushed for our iniquities;
> the punishment that brought us peace was
>   upon him,
>   and by his wounds we are healed.
> We all, like sheep, have gone astray,
>   each of us has turned to his own way;
> and the LORD has laid on him
>   the iniquity of us all. (53:5-6)

The word for *bring* has an interesting background which amplifies the idea of Jesus Christ bringing lost sinners to God. Fickett writes:

> The verb "to bring" is the Greek word *prosago* from which we get two nouns, *prosagoge* which means "right of access" and *prosagogeus* which means "introducer" or "the

giver of access." During the days when Greece was flourishing every king had a prosagogeus or an introducer. No one could have access to him except through the prosagogeus. It is through Him and only through Him that a man has access to the Almighty.[13]

Jesus punctuates the exclusive role he plays in introducing lost men and women to God in John 14:6 when he announces, "I am the way and the truth and the life. No one comes to the Father except through me." Peter, before a hostile Sanhedrin, proclaimed a corollary to this exclusivity in his reference to Jesus' name: "Salvation is found in no one else, for there is no other name under heaven given to men by which we must be saved" (Acts 4:12).

Another unique aspect of this sacrifice was its *once for all* character. This redemptive act did not feature a "built-in obsolescence"; rather, it was good for all of human history, and its effects embraced eternity. The Old Testament sacrifices which forged a temporary atonement but demanded future sacrifice were replaced by one swift divine moment when God the Father spent His Son for humanity's sins.

A Controversial Passage

The end of First Peter 3:18 details the bodily death of Jesus Christ which precedes His incredible resurrection from the dead. The section which follows, 3:19-22, has the reputation of being one of the most problematic passages in the entire New Testament.[14] The Spirit of God enabled Jesus Christ to preach to the spirits in prison, who disobeyed the message of salvation from the flood in the days of Noah.

Anyone who exegetes these verses is walking on a high wire without a safety net. The three primary questions that are applied to this passage and some frequent answers to them are charted below.

Who are the "spirits"?	When is the "proclamation"?	What is the content?
Noah's contemporaries	Interval between death/resurrection	Offer of salvation
Disobedient spirits	Pre-existent Christ preaches to Noah's contemporaries	Condemnation
	During three grave days	Those already saved

I believe that the suffering context of this passage points to a time during the three days in the grave which was a result of Jesus' unjust victimization because of sin, resulting in His crucifixion and death. Noah's contemporaries had been tendered the offer of salvation before the flood, yet they declined to accept it. It would appear that Jesus may have appeared to them with a message of condemnation to verify that they rejected the offer which would have saved them, Himself being additional verification that God honors His prophecies and promises. This serves as a tenuous opinion on a most enigmatic passage.

Peter wrote in his second letter that Paul's letters contains "some things that are hard to understand" (3:16). This difficult passage in First Peter may be also fit into the category of these "hard to understand" things.

Peter makes a link between the waters of the flood and the sacrament of baptism. The water is a symbol of baptism.[15]

Baptism is a token of salvation; it does not administer or effect salvation. It is important to note that Peter does not empower it to remove sin (1 Peter 3:21), but assigns it the role of conveying a believer's commitment and intent to obey and serve God. Without an act of faith, a dry sinner can be baptized and come out as just a wet sinner. Baptism should be an "outward profession of an inward possession"! Or, as the familiar saying goes, the ordinance is "an outward sign of an inward work of grace." Paul encapsulized the death and resurrection of Jesus Christ in the symbolism of baptism in Romans 6:3-4:

> Or don't you know that all of us who were baptized into Christ Jesus were baptized into his death? We were therefore buried with him through baptism into death in order that, just as Christ was raised from the dead through the glory of the Father, we too may live a new life.

The post-resurrection destiny of Jesus Christ is

at the Father's right hand with "angels, authorities
and powers in submission to him" (1 Peter 3:22).
The *right hand* is the symbol of authority and
power. The preeminent seat at God's right hand is
described as being reserved for Jesus Christ. Hebrews speaks of Jesus' favored position at the right
hand (emphasis added):

> The Son is the radiance of God's glory and
> the exact representation of his being, sus-
> taining all things by his powerful word. Af-
> ter he had provided purification for sins, he
> sat down at the *right hand* of the Majesty in
> heaven. (1:3)

> The point of what we are saying is this: We
> do have such a high priest, who sat down at
> the *right hand* of the throne of the Majesty in
> heaven. (8:1)

> But when this priest had offered for all time
> one sacrifice for sins, he sat down at the *right
> hand* of God. (10:12)

> Let us fix our eyes on Jesus, the author and
> perfecter of our faith, who for the joy set be-
> fore him endured the cross, scorning its
> shame, and sat down at the *right hand* of the
> throne of God. (12:2)

Yes, He suffered, but now He rules and reigns!
He is Lord of all! Our heavenly Father absorbed

our evil with His only Son. Jesus, beloved Jesus, became the sponge for the sins of the world! Sin has lost its power; it has been suffocated by the atoning Lamb of God, who suffered for wrong He did not do and gave us righteousness we could not earn or grasp!

Conclusion

Brother Lawrence remarked, "The sorest afflictions never appear intolerable, except when we see them in the wrong light."[16] The genuine disciple looks at suffering from a different corner of life's intersection. Suffering is predictable and inevitable for those who convert their theology to biography. If a person adheres to Christ's teaching, then he or she will go against the grain of the culture. Consequently, there must be splinters. Suffering can be endured if there is significance and meaning attached to the pain it shuttles into a life. Hebrews 12:2 finds significance in Jesus' stressful and painful encounter with the cross:

Let us fix our eyes on Jesus, the author and perfecter of our faith, *who for the joy set before him endured the cross,* scorning its shame, and sat down at the right hand of the throne of God (emphasis added).

Philip Brooks promoted this prayer posture which contributes to the resiliency of the believer during hard times:

Do not pray for easy lives.
Pray to be stronger men.
Do not pray for tasks equal to your powers.
Pray for powers equal to your tasks.[17]

The imperative of the deeper life enables and empowers the believer to successfully cope with the challenges of a fallen world and a hostile environment.

Discussion Questions for Further Study

1. What areas of the local church test the principle of brothers and sisters in Christ living in harmony?

2. What are some tangible evidences that a person has set apart Christ as Lord?

3. What are the reasons that you have hope in Jesus Christ?

4. How have you suffered for the cause of Jesus Christ?

5. In First Peter 3:22, Jesus Christ is at God's right hand. What impact does that have on your theology and your biography?

Endnotes

[1] Christopher J.H. Wright, *An Eye for an Eye* (Downers Grove, IL: InterVarsity Press, 1983), 198.

[2] *Finally,* in the Greek, is the word *telos,* from which we derive the English word, *teleology,* "the study of end times and events."

[3] Bruce H. Wilkinson, exec. ed., *Closer Walk* (Grand Rapids, MI: Zondervan, 1992), 215.

[4] W.E. Vine, *Expository Dictionary of New Testament Words*, 4 vols. (Grand Rapids, MI: Zondervan, 1952), Vol. 2, 239.

[5] William Barclay, *The Letters of James and Peter, The Daily Study Bible Series*, Vol. 14 (Philadelphia: Westminster Press, 1976), 225.

[6] David Augsburger, *The Freedom of Forgiveness* (Chicago: Moody, 1970), 13.

[7] Corrie Ten Boom, *Tramp for the Lord* (Old Tappan, NJ: Revell, 1974), 56-57.

[8] Edmund Burke, "Letter to William Smith," January 9, 1795.

[9] David Mains, *The Dysfunctional Church Family* (Wheaton, IL: Victor Books, 1992), 40.

[10] Philip Yancey, *Where Is God When It Hurts?* (Grand Rapids, MI: Zondervan, 1977), 176.

[11] Robert Boyd Munger, My Heart, Christ's Home (Minne-apolis, MN: Billy Graham Evangelistic Association, n. d.), 12.

[12] Oswald Chambers, quoted in *Closer Walk*, 162.

[13] Harold L. Fickett, Jr., *Peter's Principles* (Ventura, CA: Regal Books, 1974), 97.

[14] Christian tradition is divided into many camps of interpretation concerning First Peter 3:19-22. This Scripture has been utilized to support, for example, the release of confined Old Testament saints from the Limbo Patrum (Catholic), to advocate that Jesus went to hell to declare victory over the forces of darkness (Lutheran) or to provide a second chance for unbelieving spirits, resident in hell, to believe by the preaching of the good news (Anglican). These samples do not exhaust the interpretive

options. I am indebted to Dr. Elio Cuccaro for sharing ideas on this problematic passage.

15 The actual word which is translated in the NIV *symbol* is the word *antitupos*, or antitype. Barclay lends an illustrative commentary to the understanding of the antitype.

"There is *tupos*, type, which means a *seal*, and there is *antitupos*, *antitype*, which means the *impression of the seal*. Clearly, between the seal and its impression is the closest possible correspondence. So there are people and events and customs in the Old Testament which are types, and which find their antitypes in the New Testament. The Old Testament event or person is like the seal; the New Testament event or person is like the impression; the two answer each other. . . .

"Here Peter sees the bringing safely through the waters of Noah and his family as a type of baptism."—Barclay, *James and Peter*, 244.

16 Quoted in Dwight and Susan Carlson, *When Life Isn't Fair*, 169.

17 Philip Brooks, cited by Warren Wiersbe, *Why Us?* (Old Tappan, NJ: Revell, 1984), 113.

8

The Imperative of Christian Conduct in the Last Days

1 Peter 4:1-19

Therefore, since Christ suffered in his body, arm yourselves also with the same attitude, because he who has suffered in his body is done with sin. As a result, he does not live the rest of his earthly life for evil human desires, but rather for the will of God. For you have spent enough time in the past doing what pagans choose to do—living in debauchery, lust, drunkenness, orgies, carousing and detestable idolatry. They think it strange that you do not plunge with them into the same flood of dissipation, and they heap abuse on you. But they will have to give account to him who is ready to judge the living and the dead. For this is the reason the gospel was preached even to those who are now dead, so that they might be judged according to men in regard to the body, but live according to God in regard to the spirit.

The end of all things is near. Therefore be clear minded and self-controlled so that you can pray. Above all, love each other deeply, because love covers over a multitude of sins. Offer hospitality to one another without grumbling. Each one should use whatever gift he has received to serve others, faithfully administering God's grace in its various forms. If anyone speaks, he should do it as one speaking the very words of God. If anyone serves, he should do it with the strength God provides, so that in all things God may be praised through Jesus Christ. To him be the glory and the power for ever and ever. Amen.

Dear friends, do not be surprised at the painful trial you are suffering, as though something strange were happening to you. But rejoice that you participate in the sufferings of Christ, so that you may be overjoyed when his glory is revealed. If you are insulted because of the name of Christ, you are blessed, for the Spirit of glory and of God rests on you. If you suffer, it should not be as a murderer or thief or any other kind of criminal, or even as a meddler. However, if you suffer as a Christian, do not be ashamed, but praise God that you bear that name. For it is time for judgment to begin with the family of God; and if it begins with us, what will the outcome be for those who do not obey the gospel of God? And,

> *"If it is hard for the righteous to be saved,*
>   *what will become of the ungodly and the*
>   *sinner?"*

> *So then, those who suffer according to God's*
> *will should commit themselves to their faithful*
> *Creator and continue to do good.*
>   *(1 Peter 4:1-19)*

P ETER'S SERIES OF EXHORTATIONS TO his
first-century audience continue in chapter
4. His overall theme for writing the letter is
to inspire them to "stand fast" (5:12) in the mael-
strom of displacement and persecution.

Human Passions (4:1-6)

The opening "therefore" in 4:1 refers back to
3:18 which presents the suffering of Christ despite
the fact that He was the world's premiere example
of doing good. He suffered, He functioned as the
Paschal Lamb and embraced His painful journey
as the will of God.

Evan Evans, a missionary to Africa, made this
statement: "There is no Geneva Convention when
it comes to spiritual warfare." Peter frames his
challenge in the context of battle language. "Arm
yourselves," he writes in 4:1, which casts his remarks in the matrix of militancy. This analogy of
"arming" appears in several Scriptures in Pauline
literature, including:

The night is nearly over; the day is almost here. So let us put aside the deeds of darkness and put on the armor of light. (Romans 13:12)

The weapons we fight with are not the weapons of the world. On the contrary, they have divine power to demolish strongholds. (2 Corinthians 10:4)

Put on the full armor of God so that you can take your stand against the devil's schemes. (Ephesians 6:11)

Peter is referring to the weaponry of attitudes. He points his troops to the "attitude" that Jesus Christ displayed as He endured suffering at the hands of a wicked world. The believer is to have the "same mind" as the Commander-in-Chief (cf. Philippians 2:5-11). This mind-set serves Christians as they fight against the world, the flesh and the devil. The unarmed soldier, who does not understand the normalcy of suffering, will be extremely vulnerable to spiritual attack and unfair treatment.

This suffering in the body *(sarx)* has a sanctifying effect, for it fortifies a believer against sin. Peter's words, "is done with sin," denote a new power over sin and a more dynamic spiritual life which can resist it. Suffering has a redemptive influence because it makes the disciple more resilient. Without the heat of suffering, the dough cannot be made into bread! Oswald Chambers remarked, "The reason we are going through the things we are is that God wants to know whether He can make us good bread with which to feed others."[1]

Suffering has a byproduct, a result (4:2). The suffering saint who adopts the attitude of Jesus Christ is inclined to live life "for the will of God" and not "for evil human desires." Suffering prompts a person to choose the right path at the fork in the road.

God's Word often describes the two roads which face all of the human race. Psalm 1 declares there are two ways; Deuteronomy 28 provides a way of *blessing* and a way of *cursing;* Joshua chose his Master (Joshua 24:15); Jesus told of the narrow and wide gates to the road that leads to destruction or the road that leads to life (Matthew 7:13-14).

Suffering often redirects the priorities of an individual, although this is not inevitable, as evidenced by Pharaoh during the oppressive plagues brought upon Egypt. Peter taught that the negative atmosphere for the early Christians identified them with Jesus Christ and that they could capitalize on this suffering in order to live a more obedient life.

In 4:3 Peter reminds his readers of their pre-conversion scrapbook. These memories constitute a recital of sins. These pagan actions contain untamed excesses (debauchery), uncontrolled desires (lust), ungoverned consumption of wine (drunkenness), parties which violated normal levels of socialization (orgies and carousing) and disobedience of the first and second commandments (detestable idolatry). A.T. Robertson brought to the surface the frightening fact that "the Greeks actually carried lust and drunkenness into their religious observances."[2]

The issue of modeling purity in a pagan culture was a nonnegotiable for Peter. Authentic Christians are change agents who, empowered by the Holy Spirit, present a counterculture lifestyle which illustrates a marked contrast to their lifestyle in days prior to their encounter with Jesus Christ. Joseph Stowell penned a most compelling statement on the subject of purity in his book *Shepherding the Church into the 21st Century*. The President of Moody Bible Institute declares:

> Purity becomes increasingly important in contrast to our culture's disinterest in the theme. When nothing is wrong nothing is impure; guilt is unreasonable and pleasure is paramount. Yet deep within there is a hunger for a clutterless life. No matter how much permission our security grants to us to dabble in decadence, there is a residual sense of propriety that is more deeply engrained than external pressure from a fading Judeo-Christian ethic. We are image-bearers, created in His image, and hence have an intrinsic (though often buried or denied) sense that something is right and that our lives ought to be in balance with the rightness within.[3]

This U-turn in lifestyle produces bewilderment in the mind of the observing sinner. Wicked people love company and conformity. It creates a comfort level for everyone who is engaging in the same transgression. However, when a believer refuses to conform because he or she has been transformed, there is disappointment that someone has not assessed this behavior as acceptable. The Christian lifestyle is a *rebuke* of the pagan lifestyle. The dissent of the righteous becomes a platform from which abuses are directed at the nonconformist.

Jesus warned of such a reaction in this clear-cut statement in the fourth gospel: "Everyone who does evil hates the light, and will not come into the light for fear that his deeds will be exposed" (John 3:20). Light is a catalyst for fear because it exposes the darkness.

Peter details that individuals who choose a non-theistic lifestyle will have to render an account *(logon)*, or a log or diary to the Judge when the living and the dead receive the Evaluation. Virginia Cherrix, my mother-in-law, has added many new phrases to my library of quotations when our family visits her on the Eastern Shore of Virginia. One which caught my attention goes like this: "Every tub sits on its own bottom." It is true: no one will account for others, each one will give a rendering for just one person—himself!

Romans 14:12 shares the scriptural side of the colloquial expression: "So then, each of us will give an account of himself to God." Our diaries will be open to divine scrutiny, to an Almighty audit!

A.B. Simpson wrote:

> Someday we will hear our names an-
> nounced before the universe and the record
> read of things we had long forgotten. How
> our hearts will thrill, and our heads bow, as
> we hear our names called, and then the Mas-
> ter shall recount the triumph and the serv-
> ices which we had ourselves forgotten. . . .
>
> Beloved, each day we are adding to the re-
> cord of our lives. We are setting the type
> ourselves by every moment's action. Soon
> the record will be read before the audience
> of the universe and amid the issues of eter-
> nity.[4]

Peter's comments in 4:6 are very difficult to in-
terpret, but it appears that he is expanding on the
theme of 4:1-5, where he provides the options to
his readers of following human desires or God's
will (4:2). And he highlights the abuse which
comes from wicked men, because believers, who
used to engage in sinful activity, now refrain from
it because God is their ultimate environment and
they will be judged by Him (4:4-5).

In 4:6, he links this reality—men judging other
men—to the early Christians, now deceased, who
lived above human passions. Though they were
judged by men, in their earthly form ("regarding
their bodies") they possessed a dynamic force, the
presence of the Holy Spirit, which enabled them
to be men and women of spiritual integrity in the

midst of a pagan world. They lived "according to God," who is the ultimate environment and the final Judge. Indeed, Peter holds an equivalent expectation for the recipients of his letter. He uses the people of the past, transformed by the gospel, to be models for his contemporaries.

The redeemed have the honor of demonstrating what it means to be a new creation in a fallen culture. *The Book of Common Prayer* contains a number of short prayers which have inspired readers for generations. One such prayer is especially appropriate for this topic of purity in an impure world. The collect reads:

> Almighty God, you alone can bring into order the unruly wills and affections of sinners: Grant your people grace to love what you command and desire what you promise; that, among the swift and varied changes of the world, our hearts may surely be fixed where true joys are to be found; through Jesus Christ our Lord, who lives and reigns with you and the Holy Spirit, one God, now and forever. Amen.

Ethics for the End (4:7-11)

The concept of the last days is an elastic one in reference to New Testament eschatology. In the minds of the New Testament writers, the incarnation of Jesus Christ, the coming of the Messiah, is the beginning of the final era. These men projected that the end of history was imminent as evidenced by such Scriptures as:

> The night is nearly over; the day is almost here. So let us put aside the deeds of darkness and put on the armor of light. (Romans 13:12)

> Let us not give up meeting together, as some are in the habit of doing, but let us encourage one another—and all the more as you see the Day approaching. (Hebrews 10:25)

> Don't grumble against each other, brothers, or you will be judged. The Judge is standing at the door! (James 5:9)

> He who testifies to these things says, "Yes, I am coming soon."
> Amen. Come, Lord Jesus. (Revelation 22:20)

The words "is near" could read "has drawn near." Each generation expects Jesus Christ to come and bring history to its consummation. Every generation *should live* with this expectation. We are to be vigilant in watching for Him and vigorous in our ministries to promote His kingdom in this world. Every believer is to be on alert!

As with Nehemiah's workforce which rebuilt the walls of Jerusalem, we have a dual task: *working* and *watching*. A.B. Simpson observed that "God has given *us* the key to the future" in Matthew 24:14: "And this gospel of the kingdom will be preached in the whole world as a testimony to all nations, and then the end will come."[5] This posture on the end times incorporates a vigorous missionary effort. Simpson put his explanation into hymnody:

> The Master's coming draweth near,
> The Son of Man will soon appear;
>   His kingdom is at hand.
> But ere that glorious day can be,
> This gospel of the kingdom we
>   Must preach in every land.
> Oh, let us then His coming haste,
> Oh, let us end this awful waste
>   Of souls that never die.
> A thousand million still are lost,
> A Savior's blood has paid the cost,
>   Oh, hear their dying cry![6]

"Therefore," Peter states, "be clear minded and self-controlled"[7] (1 Peter 4:7). The ethics of the end times demand a sanity, a coherent mind, a lucidity of thought, so that the Christian maintains focus and faithfulness, so that distractions and temptations do not result in defections or detours from God's plan.

Exercise Self-control

As the disciple lives in the shadow of the end times there is to be the exercise of self-control. This emphasis appears two other times in the

apostle's letter. In 1:13 he exhorts his audience:
"Therefore, prepare your minds for action; be *self-controlled*; set your hope fully on the grace to be given you when Jesus Christ is revealed" (emphasis added), which links this behavior to the future event of the second coming. In his final chapter he commands self-control as a tool to enable one to defeat the adversary: "Be *self-controlled* and alert. Your enemy the devil prowls around like a roaring lion looking for someone to devour" (5:8, emphasis added).

These two disciplines—maintaining a clear mind and practicing self-control—enable the follower of Jesus Christ to be steady in uncertain and hostile times. They permit one to focus on the major functions of the faith, in particular, the discipline of *prayer* (4:7). As the child of God dialogues with the heavenly Father, spiritual stamina and resiliency are the byproducts empowering him or her to remain pure in an imperfect and decadent world.

In 4:8 Peter echoes Proverbs 10:12: "Hatred stirs up dissension, but love covers over all wrongs." The people of God, *above all*, are to "love each other deeply." The depth of this love covers a carload of sins. This word, *covers*, translates a Greek word which is used to describe muscles which are stretched to their limits, tightly drawn muscles that have been extended to their ultimate boundaries. Love is not to condone sin, but canopy over it so that its harmful effects are confined. The ethics of the end times demand adherents of the Lord Jesus who forgive and protect and restore those who fall and scrape their spiritual knees.

Elisabeth Elliot, on her national radio program, described someone who complained that a colleague committed the same error "time and time and time again." The host reminded the audience the slip occurred only three times and we are to forgive *seventy times seven*!

Practice Hospitality

Peter commends *hospitality* as another component of the end-times ethos. The word for hospitality literally means "lover of strangers." Christians traveling in the first century avoided the public inns with their pagan atmosphere and food that had already been offered to idols (cf. 1 Corinthians 8). So they would seek out a Christian home in which to stop for the night. A valuable byproduct of hospitality was that believers from widely scattered areas would get to know each other, thus cementing lines of fellowship. Thus hospitality was an important Christian virtue in that day. Even in our modern hotel-motel age it can have its place.

Hospitality was a "virtue required of the bishops and widows (1 Timothy 3:2; 5:10; Titus 1:8) and is commanded of us all (Matthew 25:35 ff.; Romans 12:13; 3 John 5-8)."[8]

Peter contends that each one should use the gift that has been received for the benefit of others in the body of Christ. The New Testament indicates that every believer has at least one gift, and some believers have multiple gifts. The three gift chapters in the New Testament are Romans 12, First Corinthians 12 and Ephesians 4. These gifts or "graces" are very diversified. Peter uses the word *poikilos, various* in the NIV. Though believers are cut from the same cloth, it has a plaid pattern. Romans 12:6 reads: "We have different gifts, according to the grace given us." The plurality of gifts are like the many different members of our human body, members which work together for a unity of purpose and fitness.

As each member uses his or her gift endowment, whether singular or plural, the body grows in its strength and usefulness. If one member is not being used or refuses to contribute to the good of the whole body, then that member is in a state of atrophy, which hurts the member and hinders the body. God gives gifts to be exercised in *body life!* A.B. Simpson wrote in *Gifts and Graces*:

> Every disciple of Christ ought to have some special manifestation of the Holy Spirit and some gift for Christian service. . . . There is no place for idlers and drones, and there is no excuse for the fruitless Christian. God has power and work for all who will yield themselves to Him for His service and glory.[9]

In his book which is customized to consider gifts, *Your Spiritual Gifts Can Help Your Church Grow*, C. Peter Wagner asserts:

Not everybody has spiritual gifts. Unbelievers do not. But every Christian person who is committed to Jesus and truly a member of His Body has at least one gift, or possibly more.[10]

Wagner defines a spiritual gift as "a special attribute given by the Holy Spirit to every member of the Body of Christ according to God's grace for use within the context of the Body."[11]

The Creator of the body has designed its function and has equipped its members to work together so that it may do great and mighty things. Congregations today, like the ones Peter addressed in the first century, have two choices: Live in harmony or die in disharmony. Charles Swindoll has a pictorial choice to frame the consequences:

Marbles or grapes, which will it be? Every congregation has a choice. You can choose to be a bag of marbles . . . independent, hard, loud, unmarked, and unaffected by others. Or, you can be a bag of grapes . . . fragrant, soft, blending, mingling, flowing into one another's lives. Marbles are made to be counted and kept. Grapes are made to be bruised and used. Marbles scar and clank. Grapes yield and cling.[12]

The expectation Peter supplies whether speaking or serving is that "God may be praised through Jesus Christ" (1 Peter 4:11). *The glory of God is the highest and most noble goal of Christian words or works!* The Christian is to join the chorus sung by the four and twenty elders who sing: "You are worthy, our Lord and God, to receive glory and honor and power, for you created all things, and by your will they were created and have their being" (Revelation 4:11). Bob Kilpatrick wrote a contemporary chorus with a comparable theme:

"Lord, Be Glorified"

In my life, Lord,
Be glorified, be glorified.
In my life, Lord,
Be glorified today.

In your church, Lord,
Be glorified, be glorified.
In your church, Lord,
Be glorified today.[13]

Suffering in God's Will (1 Peter 4:12-19)

No other topic is more recycled in Peter's letter than the suffering of the believer. In this passage Peter revisits the premise that suffering is the *normal expectation* for those who pursue God's will and who seek to walk in the footprints of Jesus Christ. These first-century mariners were navigating through stormy waters. Peter perceives suffering to be an inevitable consequence of Christian living. This is to be no surprise that painful trials would be part of their diary. The Greek adjective for painful is *purosis,* which literally means "burning." This suffering brings uncomfortable heat and singes the clothes and sometimes brings third-degree burns to the flesh of life. Earlier in his letter, Peter had instructed his readers that "These have come so that your faith—of greater worth than gold, which perishes even though refined by fire—may be proved genuine and may result in praise, glory and honor when Jesus Christ is revealed" (1:7).

Many contemporary Christians need to understand this nonnegotiable: Christians will suffer *because of* their faith. This requires some individuals to make a paradigm shift, for they accepted Jesus Christ as an insurance policy, believing that He would wrap insulation around them and they would be spared any pain, discomfort, inconvenience or rejection. However, the symbol of Christianity is not a pillow but a *cross!* A.B. Simpson made this observation:

> Most persons after a step of faith are looking for sunny skies and unruffled seas, and when they meet a storm and tempest they are filled with astonishment and perplexity. But this is just what we must expect to meet if we have received anything of the Lord. The best token of His presence is the adversary's defiance. The more real our blessing,

the more certainly it will be challenged. It is
a good thing to go out looking for the worst,
and if it comes we are not surprised.[14]

William Penn, the Quaker, declared: "no cross,
no crown."[15] Peter's scouting report is relevant for
every Christian. We should anticipate that suffering will be inclusive for the people of God. The
disciple who does not experience some degree of
suffering is an aberration of the Christian faith!

Peter contends that suffering and rejoicing are
not mutually exclusive. In fact, they are compat-
ible. The New Testament provides ample ammunition to this thesis. Acts 5:41 reports: "The
apostles left the Sanhedrin, rejoicing because they
had been counted worthy of suffering disgrace for
the Name." Acts 16:25 depicts two incarcerated
Christians in a festive mood: "About midnight
Paul and Silas were praying and singing hymns to
God, and the other prisoners were listening to
them." Paul went so far as to aspire to suffer: "I
want to know Christ and the power of his resurrection and the fellowship of sharing in his sufferings, becoming like him in his death" (Philippians
3:10).

This is not Stoic philosophy which declares fate
demands that we suffer. Nor is it masochism
which asserts, "I enjoy suffering." Rather it is pur-
poseful suffering which the heavenly Father permits and sometimes plans, so that His perfect will
may be accomplished. Christians must have the
long view of life.

Stephen Covey, who wrote *Seven Habits of Highly Effective People,* includes this principle, "Begin with the end in mind."[16] If we begin the Christian life understanding that we will be honored beyond imagination and realize that when we are suffering we are accomplishing *eternal work,* then we will react much differently when we are burnt by its flames. When suffering comes, we must submit our impulsive distaste for discomfort to the higher value of glorifying God and honoring Jesus Christ. The Master left us this legacy, "Let us fix our eyes on Jesus, the author and perfecter of our faith, who for the joy set before him endured the cross, scorning its shame, and sat down at the right hand of the throne of God" (Hebrews 12:2). The believer is to be "cool in the furnace."

Christianity contains a long list of paradoxes, including "the last shall be first," "the least shall be greatest," "the weak shall be the strong." Another paradoxical principle resides in First Peter 4:14: "insult equals blessing." This is contingent upon the insult stemming as a result of the name and cause of Jesus Christ. Insult was common fare in the daily diet of many Christians. Yet for the Christian it became a catalyst for God's glorious Spirit to rest upon his or her life!

Suffering is not commended for non-Christian acts such as murder, theft, meddling or other criminal violations (4:15). There is to be no duplicity—living in two worlds, being a double agent or a spiritual schizophrenic, bouncing between light and darkness.

"However, if you suffer as a Christian," Peter instructs in 4:16, "do not be ashamed, but praise God that you bear that name." Quite a mouthful from someone who had denied Jesus when his life was jeopardized during the dark agony of his Lord's trial and torture! Peter had learned from his failure, and later would manifest courage and resolve during the dynamic growth of the early Church which was coupled with a plurality of persecutions.

His advice had emerged from his own successful coping with conflict and the personal pain which he experienced.

The term "Christian" appears *three times* in the New Testament (Acts 11:26; Acts 26:28; 1 Peter 4:16). Billy Graham made this connection:

> In each of these instances the idea of suffering and persecution is in the context. No, Christ does not promise that all is going to be easy and trouble-free for us. By and large, the totally committed Christians have been a suffering people, a persecuted people. Yes, it costs to follow Christ; but if you have glimpsed the glory of what God has done for us, no price is too great to pay to declare His glory.[17]

In 4:17-18, Peter makes a clear-cut distinction between the family of God (the righteous) and the disobedient (the ungodly sinner). The degree of judgment will be more severe for those who have not embraced the gospel. The members of God's family do experience judgment and hardship on earth. Moses and David serve as two classic examples. Sometimes judgment is brought on by the sinful activity of those who serve God; at other times the judgment is imposed on the believer by those who are anti-Christian. Peter's point is this: If the family member experiences judgment, you can expect a greater pain and penalty for those who have rejected God's offer of salvation and who have ignored His Word.

The audience that Peter was addressing is instructed to commit to a faithful Creator and to persist in good works, even though suffering and hardship have touched their lives. The authentic disciple must come to terms with God's sovereignty, His absolute control over success and sorrow.

The word for *commit* is *parathesthai* which Barclay translates as "depositing money with a trusted friend."[18] This is the same word which Jesus used from the cross when he exclaimed with a loud voice, "Father, into your hands I commit my spirit" (Luke 23:46). It also appears in Second Timothy 2:2: "And the things you have heard me say in the presence of many witnesses entrust *(parathesthai)* to reliable men who will also be qualified to teach others." To commit is to invest something of worth and merit to the care and discretion of another.

This is no marshmallow task; it is accepting God's will, even when it is thorny and difficult, even if it means the sacrifice of earthly life for heavenly gain! The Christian becomes *God's visual aid*, demonstrating a higher ethic and an eternal perspective.

One respected devotional writer has observed:

> To choose to suffer means there is something wrong. To choose God's will even if it means suffering is a very different thing. No healthy saint ever chooses suffering; he chooses God's will, as Jesus did, whether it means suffering or not.[19]

Walter Williams shared this vignette in his volume on Quaker history. George Fox and the Quakers were having phenomenal success in seventeenth-century England as they preached the gospel. However, in the process of this great revival Fox was arrested for blasphemy. Placed in a filthy dungeon, full of vermin and villains, he was not permitted to have visitors. One hundred fifty miles away a sixteen-year-old cripple named James Parnell heard about Fox's dilemma and made the long journey to the prison. He found a window of opportunity and was able to meet with George Fox. Williams records this assessment:

> After he and George Fox spent some time in fellowship together, the lad left Carlisle dungeon with heart aflame, and gave the rest of his life to the Friends' Movement.[20]

We must allow God to choose the soil in which we are planted. Some species produce in fine, lush soil; others can manifest fruit in limestone and clay soil. He chooses our place; we choose His will!

Conclusion

Living the deeper life does not mean looking at Christianity as one more insurance policy. There are no guarantees that the believer will be exempt from snowstorms and floods. This passage in particular allows for good works to be rewarded with harsh reaction. To obey God is often to offend society. Missionaries have endured some of the most flagrant exhibitions of mistreatment. They leave their country and kindred to assist in the evangelization and rebuilding of another culture, but they are often greeted with disrespect and disdain.

I remember hearing a leader of Co-Mission share with a congregation that in Russia, the general populace will listen more readily to the gray-haired missionary than the novice missionary. He observed that the Russians, who have been subject to brutal suffering and oppression, place much more credibility in the tested and tried life, in the person who knows what it means to walk through rugged terrain.

As Christians submit to suffering, they may be earning the right to be heard by a suspicious and cautious world. Suffering may provide the platform for a fair hearing of the gospel.

Discussion Questions for Further Study

1. Reread 4:8. Who are some people in your local church that you love deeply?

2. What are some opportunities to exercise hospitality?

3. How many spiritual gifts can you discover in these chapters? 1 Corinthians 12, Romans 12 and Ephesians 4? (Try to list at least ten.)

4. What do you believe are your spiritual gifts? How are you using them?

5. Can you name someone who died for his or her Christian stand?

Endnotes

1 Oswald Chambers, *Daily Thoughts for Disciples* (Grand Rapids, MI: Zondervan, 1990), 94.

2 Archibald Thomas Robertson, *Word Pictures in the New Testament, The General Epistles and the Revelation of John*, Vol. 6 (Grand Rapids, MI: Baker, 1933), 122.

3 Joseph M. Stowell, *Shepherding the Church into the 21st Century* (Wheaton, IL: Victor Books, 1994), 190.

4 A.B. Simpson, *Days of Heaven on Earth* (Camp Hill, PA: Christian Publications, 1984), August 1.

5 A.B. Simpson, *Missionary Messages* (Camp Hill, PA: Christian Publications, 1987), 25.

6 Ibid., 25-26.

7 The word for "clear-minded" is illuminated by William Barclay: "The verb Peter uses is *sophronein*; connected with that verb is the noun *sophrosune*, which the Greeks derived from the verb *sozein, to keep safe*, and the noun

phronesis, the mind. Sophrosune is the wisdom which characterizes a man who is preeminently sane; and *sophronein* means *to preserve one's sanity.*"—William Barclay, *The Letters of James and Peter, The Daily Study Bible Series,* Vol. 14 (Philadelphia: Westminster Press, 1976), 251.

[8] Leon Morris, et. al., *Hebrews-Revelation, The Expositor's Bible Commentary,* Vol. 12, ed. Frank E. Gaebelein (Grand Rapids, MI: Zondervan, 1981), 246.

[9] A.B. Simpson, *Gifts and Graces* (Camp Hill, PA: Christian Publications, 1993), 3.

[10] C. Peter Wagner, *Your Spiritual Gifts Can Help Your Church Grow* (Ventura, CA: Regal Books, 1979), 39.

[11] Ibid., 142.

[12] Charles R. Swindoll, *The Quest for Character* (Portland, OR: Multnomah Press, 1987), 144.

[13] Bob Kilpatrick, "Lord, Be Glorified" (Prism Tree Music, 1978).

[14] A.B. Simpson, *Days of Heaven on Earth,* September 13th.

[15] William Penn, "No Cross, No Crown," 1669.

[16] Stephen R. Covey, *Seven Habits of Highly Effective People* (New York: Simon and Schuster, 1989), 95.

[17] Billy Graham, "No Retreat," *Decision,* July 1977.

[18] Barclay, *James and Peter,* 261.

[19] Oswald Chambers, quoted in Bruce H. Wilkinson, exec. ed., *Closer Walk* (Grand Rapids, MI: Zondervan, 1992), 343.

[20] Paul S. Rees, *The Epistles to the Philippians, Colossians and Philemon* (Grand Rapids, MI: Baker, 1964), 31.

9

The Imperative to Elders

1 Peter 5:1-4

To the elders among you, I appeal as a fellow elder, a witness of Christ's sufferings and one who also will share in the glory to be revealed: Be shepherds of God's flock that is under your care, serving as overseers—not because you must, but because you are willing, as God wants you to be; not greedy for money, but eager to serve; not lording it over those entrusted to you, but being examples to the flock. And when the Chief Shepherd appears, you will receive the crown of glory that will never fade away. (1 Peter 5:1-4)

THE FIFTH CHAPTER OF FIRST PETER is one of the most important passages on the subject of leadership in the entire Bible. The apostle was highly qualified to lecture on leadership. Peter had been discipled by Jesus, observed His methods, tested them in the laboratory of human experience and lived long enough at the writing of this epistle to verify their validity.

The first four verses are worth their weight in gold, for they share the primary functions of leadership as well as the motivations which are essential for pleasing the Lord and also for the fulfilling of the criteria that Christ Jesus will use for the disbursements of final rewards.

Every church leader, pastoral or lay, will benefit immensely as he or she understands the mind of God on leadership and applies these principles with a divine attitude and ethos. We can avoid the dilemma of the hunter who shot his gun and then ran into the field to see if he had hit anything. This passage of Scripture allows us to aim that we may hit the mark!

An Equal Elder (5:1)

First Peter 5:1 identifies the writer's position in the church and the recipients of his message. It is essential to observe that Peter puts himself on the same level as those he is addressing. He has targeted the elders for some didactic exhortation on their role in the church, and he has labeled himself as a fellow-elder.

The church must realize that the Lord does not see all the hierarchy of importance that we sometimes presume is built into the titles that we hold. The Scriptures are very clear in assessing all believers as priests in the work of God. This concept emerged during the days of Israel's captivity and exodus from Egypt, and is prominent in New Testament writings (Exodus 19:6; 1 Peter 2:5, 9).

There is a *parity* in our positions as believers and as church leaders, because God has equipped us and is working in all of us. The distinctions of clergy and laity are helpful, but they have often led the people of God on a detour of distinction that the Lord has not chosen. Peter, one of the original twelve disciples of Jesus, the chosen mouthpiece of God for the sermon on the day of Pentecost at which 3,000 were converted, has espoused an equality with the elders of these upstart churches in Asia Minor.

The term for *elder* in 5:1 is the word which we have anglicized into *presbyter*. The primary usage in the New Testament is the description of those who were ruling leaders in a local assembly. These elders were specifically recognized and set apart to minister to the young churches in the first-century world that were springing up with rapid frequency under the domination of the Roman Empire. This term, *presbyter*, is still used as a designation in many denominations.

Before we depart 5:1, it is necessary to notice that Peter includes a prize, a dangling golden carrot, before the mind of the reader. He is planning to be a partaker of the glory to be revealed, and before this section of Scripture is closed, he will come full circle to this theme in reference to the elders that he is exhorting. God's leaders, who do His work and perform it in His way, have the rea-

sonable expectation of heavenly horizons and reward ceremonies.

A Servant/Shepherd (5:2-3)

The second verse of this text cites a metaphor
which is indispensable in conceptualizing Christian leadership. A metaphor is presented of shepherding the flock of God. As the verse unfolds
there are two distinct types of care that the shepherd must attend to, namely, (1) *personal care*,
which is hands-on ministry, addressing basic and
immediate needs of the sheep and (2) the shepherd
must *plan ahead and prepare* for the future needs of
the sheep, and he must execute supervision over
the care of the sheep, which is less direct and less
personal. The first set of duties might be classified
as *pastoral*, while the second set of duties might be
classified as *administrative*. The effective leader of
any ministry, church, district or denomination
must pursue both of these functions simultane-
ously. If a pastor puts only one oar in the water,
the boat will not move forward, but in circles. It is
expedient that both the pastoral oar and the administrative oar be rowed at the same time.

A third primary function will surface in verse 3,
that of (3) *discipleship by modeling*.

A shepherd cannot sit in his office and neglect
the basic needs of his flock. You cannot read the
Twenty-third Psalm and not be impressed by the
very personal nature of the Shepherd's care. As
men and women assume leadership over God's
sheep, whether it be in large units such as denomi-

nations, district or churches, or in small units such as classes, choirs and committees, there must be close and responsive relational care exercised to those who the leader is responsible for and working with so that the flock is kept functioning and productive.

There are many aspects to personal, pastoral care. A few primary functions that emerge are leading, feeding, protecting, healing, rebuking and encouraging. To fulfill these duties effectively the leader of a group must be *in touch* with those to whom he has been assigned.

In the book entitled *Habits of the Heart*, written by four sociologists and one philosopher, the thesis is presented that American society is moving away from community activity to more individual activity.[1] We are withdrawing from each other, the authors contend, and the thesis is also applied to the Church as it seeks to minister to the world. That thesis can be preached to many churches about their internal structure. The Word of God makes many assertions about our horizontal care and love to each other. The phrase "our brother's keeper" is a biblical phrase.

The second thrust of leadership in this verse is that of overseeing or administration. The word in the Greek, when anglicized, is *episcopal*. We have derived the concept of bishop from this word— one who exercises supervision and administrates in a broader, long-distance sense. Good leaders not only minister for the moment in tender ways, they also oversee and anticipate in more long-term decision making. This aspect of church leadership is sadly deficient in the contemporary church. It has left the church giving knee-jerk reactions to discipleship, music, building programs, finances—indeed, every facet of the church has been affected.

The critical point is this: Ministers who ignore either pastoral or administrative care are ministers who limp and stumble and eventually do not bring glory to God. Ministers who address both immediate needs and supervisory needs are usually those who are less problematic and more productive.

This verse exposes another facet of leadership, for the issues of actions are also coupled with attitude. What are the motivations which accompany our service as leaders? It is very possible to be doing the right thing for the wrong reason, and apparently there were those in the first-century Church who struggled with this issue. It is apparent from reading the New Testament that some lost the battle.

The contrasts are very graphic concerning motivational forces which affect leadership. The first is a question of will: "not because you must, but because you are willing." Whose will is behind your leadership? Is it you exercising free will to be involved, or has some other person or group prevailed with their will? God's will is that leaders are not functioning by coercion or compulsion, but rather because they want to do the job! One of the fundamental challenges for any local church is to assist people in the discovery of their gifts, to place them in the Body of Christ so that they are doing the things God equipped them to do. Often people are forced into positions and functions that are far removed from God's intentions. The other side of the issue is the gifted individual whose spiritual life is at low tide and who doesn't care to invest his or her gift for God. Ability is not enough to serve in God's kingdom!

The second issue is as up-to-date as today's newspaper. Are you serving for selfish reasons? Are you striving so that you may gain personally? The emphasis in the text is monetary—"not greedy for money, but eager to serve" (5:2). The ministry today is a real test of motivation. The breezes of materialism have blown into the pastor's study, and the temptation is to become a *mercenary* rather than a *minister* of God. The sense of call to a church has often become "dollars and cents." This is just one example of the motivational struggle. There are other issues.

Some aspire to church leadership because they want to control or show-off or have their names published or beef up their résumés. Personal ambitions can be very devilish. Peter does not applaud "lording it over those entrusted to you" (5:3). Stephen Neill, one of the most prominent missionary writers in the twentieth century, was speaking to young ministers about to be ordained. He shared his thoughts on personal gain:

I am inclined to think that ambition in any
ordinary sense of the term is nearly always
sinful in ordinary men. I am certain that in
the Christian it is always sinful, and that it is
most inexcusable of all in the ordained minister.[2]

All of us are aware of God's omniscience, His
complete knowledge of the thoughts and intents of
the heart. A leader may fool the people, but God
will not be mocked. The phrase "ready mind" in
the KJV, "eager to serve" in the NIV, and
"eagerly" in the RSV, are the translations of a
word which literally means *forward spirit*. The
godly leader is like a race horse at the gate ready
to be set free to run for His owner. Leadership
should not be a drag, but a delight. Leadership
should not be coerced but should be rendered
with celebration.

"Power and position corrupt, and absolute
power and position corrupt absolutely." Christianity has turned the topic of leadership upside
down. In our culture and in many others, the
higher you go, the more people serve you. In
Christ, the higher you go, the more people you
have to serve. Here, the Church becomes a counterculture to the world of business and the world-
at-large.

We preach not the "gospel of get" but the "gospel of give." Our inspiration for such a statement
comes directly from the lips of our Lord Jesus. He
said in Matthew 20:28: "the Son of Man did not

come not to be served, but to serve, and to give his life as a ransom for many."

On the eve of His crucifixion, He stripped down, girded Himself with a towel, washed the grimy feet of His disciples and then stated: "I have set you an example that you should do as I have done for you" (John 13:15). In Matthew 23:11-12, His description of greatness is so different from what we are conditioned to believe: "The greatest among you will be your servant. For whoever exalts himself will be humbled, and whoever humbles himself will be exalted."

The life of Jesus Christ is a breathtaking "video" of the servant lifestyle. As district licensing and ordination committees and local church search committees participate in the selection of leaders in the church, it is critical that they assign deference to those that are servants. One has written:

> Because we children of Adam
>   want to become great,
>   He became small.
> Because we will not stoop,
>   He humbled Himself.
> Because we want to rule,
>   He came to serve.[3]

We lead most effectively by our example. This is discipleship by modeling. Paul used this method in his training of Timothy. In Paul's final letter from a Roman prison cell he communicates this powerful charge to his apprentice:

You, however, know all about my teaching,
my way of life, my purpose, faith, patience,
love, endurance, persecutions, sufferings—
what kinds of things happened to me in An-
tioch, Iconium and Lystra, the persecutions
I endured. Yet the Lord rescued me from all
of them. (2 Timothy 3:10-11)

Paul does not emphasize the teaching that he
has done with his lips but rather the teaching he
has done with his life. He has visibly demonstrated the living power of Jesus Christ in his life.
His chief mentoring has occurred through his actions and reactions to people and circumstances.

Discipleship is most indelibly registered by
those who follow as they actually see a genuine
fleshing out of what we have preached and
taught. The leader's theology must be translated
into biography! "Do as I say, not as I do," is the
pathetic axiom of an anemic leader. "Imitate me
as I imitate the Lord Jesus Christ" is the dynamic challenge of a man or woman of God! As
we walk in His steps, others will follow Him by
following us.

Stephen Julian, one of the pastors I served with
on a church staff, had a motto placed on his desk
which is mostly true: "Youth need models, not
critics!" John Maxwell endorsed the discipleship-
by-modeling a principle in his book *The Winning
Attitude:* "The greatest of motivational principles
is: People do what people see. As adults we are
still playing follow the leader."[4]

Chief Shepherd (5:4)

You have heard the terms *bishop* and *archbishop*, and you understand that one takes precedence over the other. In 5:4, as this segment of Scripture wraps itself up, the insertion of a new term is found in the label of *archshepherd*, or in our vernacular, *Chief Shepherd.* This is indispensable to a proper concept of the Church. Jesus is the Head of the Church universal, but He is also Head of the church local. The pastors nor the elders nor the governing board nor the congregational meeting are ultimate in the church. All of these people groups bow low before Jesus Christ!

One of the functions of this Archshepherd is to reward His undershepherds. It is the recognition banquet of heaven, and the leaders are summoned before Him. There we will realize more fully what it means to be partakers of glory. There Jesus will distribute the crowns that we sing about so often in our hymns.

It is an unfading crown. It does not burn up or rust; it is indestructible. The word in the original is one that is used to name a flower, *amaranth*, which never seems to wilt; but if it does, a little spray of water can revive it. This is an eternal trophy that Jesus Christ will grant the leaders of His Church.

I do want one of those crowns. I hope to receive one. How about you? The apostle Paul highlighted the reception of this crown near the end of his final letter: "Now there is in store for me the crown of righteousness, which the Lord, the righteous Judge, will award to me on that day—and not only to me, but also to all who have longed for his appearing" (2 Timothy 4:8).

Every leader is the shepherd of a flock. To this person has been assigned the task of pastoral and administrative care. In this person's life should be transcribed the very life of Christ. To this person who aspires and achieves a crown will be given more precious than any earthly trinket of triumph.

Leadership, in the Spirit of Jesus Christ, is the heartbeat of a New Testament Church. He is the Good Shepherd, and every elder is an undershepherd. The Good Shepherd spent His life for the sheep, not vice versa. This is a paradox, for the average sheep lives for the profit of the shepherd and is ultimately sacrificed for his gain. The biblical model turns this upside down—the Christian shepherd surrenders his life for the sheep's profit. Jesus left us the pattern. His eldership meant sacrifice of the greatest degree. He gave Himself. Every elder must understand the terms of his contract.

Conclusion

A young coast guard recruit was called along with his crew to attempt a desperate rescue in a terrible storm. Frightened, rain pounding like pellets in his face, he cried to his captain, "We will never get back!"

The captain replied, "We don't have to come back, but we must go out."[5]

The authentic shepherd places his life in jeopardy for the sheep and sometimes *spends it* for the safety, security and survival of his flock.

As I reach for a personal illustration to illustrate the elder who is willing, eager to serve and an example, my mind recalls a pinewood derby which was held at a local church. I was present on a Saturday morning because my son Marc particpated in his first ever pinewood race.

Our elders had started an urban ministry in a nearby metropolitan area. They traveled to the city an extra night each week to give the gospel of Jesus Christ to those who had not heard and whose lives were tainted with sin. I discovered that several of our elders had transported a large electric saw into the inner city so that these boys would be able to participate in the pinewood derby. They found special scales so that the cars which were made would not exceed the five-ounce limit. These men had helped to design and paint these vehicles, and some of them won trophies that day because of their speed or appearance.

As I observed those men I saw Jesus personified. Yes, they had burnt time, gasoline and energy in an attempt to demonstrate Christ's love to these young men. But I witnessed willing hearts and eager hands and men who looked so proud and tall because they had assisted these children.

That pinewood derby had defined for me the eldership that Peter wrote about in First Peter 5:4.

Those elders had *made the invisible Christ visible* to young men in Akron, Ohio.

Discussion Questions for Further Study

1. Who are the elders in your local church? When is the last time you prayed for their shepherding ministry? (Perhaps now is as good a time as any.)

2. What are three distinguishing characteristics of good shepherds as revealed in this short passage?

3. What are the qualifications for elder in your church? How do those compare to the characteristics in this passage?

4. Who is the Chief Shepherd and what does He give?

Endnotes

1 Robert Bellah, et. al., *Habits of the Heart* (Berkeley, CA: University of California Press, 1985).

2 Stephen Neill, "Address to Ordinands," *The Record,* March 28, 1947, 161.

3 J. Oswald Sanders, rev. ed. *Spiritual Leadership* (Chicago: Moody Press, 1994), 16.

4 John C. Maxwell, *The Winning Attitude* (San Bernadino, CA: Here's Life Publishers, 1992), 169.

5 J. Oswald Sanders, *Spiritual Leadership* (Chicago: Moody Press, 1994), 59.

10

The Imperative of
Suffering a Little While

1 Peter 5:5-11

Young men, in the same way be submissive to those who are older. All of you, clothe yourselves with humility toward one another, because,

> *"God opposes the proud*
> *but gives grace to the humble."*

Humble yourselves, therefore, under God's mighty hand, that he may lift you up in due time. Cast all your anxiety on him because he cares for you.

Be self-controlled and alert. Your enemy the devil prowls around like a roaring lion looking for someone to devour. Resist him, standing firm in the faith, because you know that your brothers throughout the world are undergoing the same kind of sufferings.

> *And the God of all grace, who called you to*
> *his eternal glory in Christ, after you have suf-*
> *fered a little while, will himself restore you and*
> *make you strong, firm and steadfast. To him be*
> *the power for ever and ever. Amen. (1 Peter*
> *5:5-11)*

PETER HAS WOVEN INTO HIS letter a recital of submission scenarios, including: submitting to government authorities (2:13-17); submitting to employers (2:18-20); wives submitting to husbands (3:1-6); and undershepherds (elders) submitting to the Chief Shepherd (5:1-4). He now addresses younger men and their obligation to submit to older men (5:5). The younger men are to *exercise generational etiquette!*

Submission in Suffering (5:5-7)

This teaching is wrapped in a passage which is devoted to the humility which permits a child of God to submit to suffering. The word for *humility, tapeinophrosune,* could be translated "lowliness of mind." This is a counterculture trait. Society is infatuated with "high-mindedness" and bookstores are saturated with manuals on climbing the corporate and societal ladders. But the Christian is to include *humility* in his or her wardrobe.

The phrase "clothe yourself with humility" actually refers to a slave putting on an apron prior to serving.[1] The phrase "toward one another" places this command within the sphere of believers and their attitudes toward other believers. This is not to be a one-way street, but a mutual expression freely and consistently expressed between brothers and sisters in God's family. Peter incorporates a quote from Proverbs 3:34: "He mocks proud mockers but gives grace to the humble." Humility is related to submissiveness. The self-assertive posture is to be replaced by a servant's humility.

The chorus of the disciple of Jesus Christ should be "I Exalt Thee," not "I Exalt Me." Yet as the believer exalts the Lord, personal exaltation will transpire—"that he may lift you up in due time" (1 Peter 5:6). Peter marries humility and eschatology. The humble Christian can expect to be elevated in God's timetable, "the fullness of time." The lowering of oneself is a down payment on the promotion of one's status in the kingdom of God in days to come. Jesus explicitly endorsed this thesis in Luke 14:11: "For everyone who exalts himself will be humbled, and he who humbles himself will be exalted." Can I trust God to exalt me in His time? Philippians 2:5-11 beautifully portrays the humiliation of Jesus which preceded His honor and exaltation:

Your attitude should be the same as that of Christ Jesus:

Who, being in very nature God,
    did not consider equality with God
        something to be grasped,

but made himself nothing,
   taking the very nature of a servant,
   being made in human likeness.
And being found in appearance as a man,
   he humbled himself
   and became obedient to death—
     even death on a cross!
Therefore God exalted him to the highest
     place
  and gave him the name that is above every
     name,
that at the name of Jesus every knee should
     bow,
  in heaven and on earth and under the
     earth,
and every tongue confess that Jesus Christ is
     Lord,
   to the glory of God the Father.

I was taught a lesson in humility and holiness by a man who has won many art and book awards. When I approached him about working on a project with me, he unintentionally instructed me in "spiritual mathematics" when he told me that he did not want royalties, only a per-item fee for his artwork. Also, he told me that my name should be larger than his on the cover. He knows how to count, but not necessarily dollars and cents or recognition and visibility. He is competent in counting me as a higher number than himself.

His response made me think twice about how I

approach projects and situations where I can choose to be noticed or remain in the background. I will not forget his holy humility. He "made the invisible Christ visible" for me on the phone that day in 1995. He could have asked for his name of equal billing or larger (and the publisher would have been thrilled, because he is known and I am not). He could have demanded that he have a larger share of the royalties, but he didn't. What he did demand was my attention; what he did cause was my conviction. His counting was like Jesus Christ!

Psalm 75:7 gives reinforcement to the parabolic curve of God's assessment: "But it is God who judges: He brings one down, he exalts another." This demands *faith in the sovereignty of God.* The eyes must look beyond the obvious to the actual.

The humble posture is rare in any generation. Nevertheless, it is an assumed normative by the biblical writers. Because of its infrequency, it stands out prominently when it is demonstrated. One such occasion is noted in the diary of Samuel Brengle when he was introduced as "the great Doctor Brengle":

> If I appear great in their eyes, the Lord is most graciously helping me to see how absolutely nothing I am without Him, and helping me to keep little in my own eyes. He does use me. But I am so concerned that He uses me and that it is not of me the work is

done. The ax cannot boast of the trees it has cut down. It could do nothing but for the woodsman. He made it, he sharpened it, and he used it. The moment he throws it aside, it becomes only old iron. O that I may never lose sight of that.[2]

Samuel Brengle had the John-the-Baptist mindset: "He must become greater; I must become less" (John 3:30). This is the Lord's expectation for His children.

Christian counselors are partial to the potency of First Peter 5:7: "Cast all your anxiety on him because he cares for you." Dependence is more Christian than independence. The practice of casting our cares on God is one of the most potent acts of humility. To cast, to throw upon the Lord our anxieties is an actualization of our inadequacy without Him. The original word for anxiety is *mermimna* which means *to divide*. Those who attempt to manage all of their stress and all of their burdens become overwhelmed by the load. They become unstable, distracted, self-absorbed.

The Lord prescribes a remedy: "Cast your cares," "alleviate your anxieties," "download your dilemmas." Why? "Because He cares for you." The Mighty God, the Majestic God is personal and compassionate to the smallest specimen of humanity. He cares! He tenders a standing offer to His people, "Cast your cares; please don't hoard them; cast them!"

A.W. Tozer, when writing of this Christian

benefit of care-casting, donated this counsel: "Remember that peace of heart does not come from denying there is trouble, but comes from rolling your trouble on God."[3]

The Advocate of Suffering (5:8-9)

Red alert! Being humble during suffering will prepare the believer to face the stiff winds of an adversary. The attitude that accompanies this virtue works to counter overconfidence in the battle which occurs between the saint and the predator of the saints. A.W. Tozer contributes these insights to the encounter with the devil: "I stand for believing in God and defying the devil—and our God loves that kind of courage among His people."[4]

It is our faith in a mighty God, and not a smug self-sufficiency, that dares to resist and conquer the opponent. Like David, the humble Christian replies, "The battle is the Lord's."

The enemy, the devil, is on the prowl like a hungry lion stalking his prey. The word for *devil, diabolos,* is the Greek translation of the Hebrew *Satan*. These words portray this evil one as a slanderer, a false accuser. The biblical record speaks highly of this antagonist. He is powerful; he is cunning. He is successful in the short run. Billy Graham corrects the spin that has underestimated this worthy opponent:

> Modern confusion about the personality
> of the devil has resulted in large measure

from the caricatures of him which became popular during the Middle Ages. To allay their fear of the devil, people tried to laugh at him, and pictured him as a foolish, grotesque creature with horns and a long tail. They put a pitchfork in his hand, and a feeble-minded leer on his face. . . .

We forget that the devil was perhaps the greatest and most exalted of all of God's angels. He was a sublime figure, who decided to use his divine endowments for his own aims instead of God's. His reasoning is brilliant, his plans ingenious, his logic well nigh irrefutable. God's mighty adversary is no bungling creature with horns and tail—he is a prince of lofty stature, of unlimited craft and cunning, able to take advantage of every opportunity that presents itself, able to turn every situation to his own advantage. He is unrelenting and cruel. He is not, however, all powerful, omniscient or omnipresent.[5]

It is important to note that the word for *enemy* is *antidikos* which could be translated, "the opponent in a lawsuit." Years ago, in the early days of television, Raymond Burr played the part of a defense attorney named Perry Mason. This lawyer never lost a case for his client. At times, Warren Burger, the prosecuting attorney, seemed to have the case wrapped up tight, but Perry Mason always found a way to win.

Jesus Christ is our Advocate (1 John 2:1); He is

our spiritual Perry Mason. We cannot lose if He is representing us—and He is! Though the devil is an advocate of the believer's suffering, his influence and power are nullified by the premiere Advocate, Jesus Christ.

The devil has a short-term lease on his authority. He is the prince of this world (John 14:30), but Jesus is the King. The fate which awaits him is clarified in the Bible's final book:

> The great dragon was hurled down—that ancient serpent called the devil, or Satan, who leads the whole world astray. He was hurled to the earth, and his angels with him.
> Then I heard a loud voice in heaven say:
>
> "Now have come the salvation and the
>   power and the kingdom of our God,
>   and the authority of his Christ.
> For the accuser of our brothers,
>   who accuses them before our God day
>   and night,
>   has been hurled down.
> They overcame him
>   by the blood of the Lamb
>   and by the word of their testimony;
> they did not love their lives so much
>   as to shrink from death.
>   (Revelation 12:9-11)

The apostle champions an active resistance. "Resist him, standing firm in the faith" (1 Peter

5:9). James 4:7 also promotes this proactive stance: "Submit yourselves, then, to God. *Resist* the devil, and he will flee from you" (emphasis added). Again, as in Peter's epistle, submission to God is coupled with resistance to the devil.

Jesus displayed a primary weapon in this spiritual warfare. When confronted by this same devil during temptation in the wilderness, the Master Warrior retreated to the Scriptures *three times* and successfully countered three separate attacks. Another aspect of the arsenal is prayer. Jesus commended this resource to His disciples in the Garden of Gethsemane, Mark 14:38, "Watch and pray so that you will not fall into temptation. The spirit is willing, but the body is weak."

Also, Peter mentions that suffering is not just limited to his readers, but there is a solidarity of suffering saints around the world. Suffering creates an atmosphere of isolation, but in real terms there is no island of suffering. Rather, the members of God's family in all nations, in all generations, of all races and genders and ages vicariously encounter suffering and are challenged and commanded to stand fast. There is to be no turning back, no retreat. When Cortes landed in Mexico in 1518 he ordered his men to burn the ships which brought them so that retreat was not possible. The Christian must burn his bridges and ships so that there is a commitment to accomplish the mission!

Restoration in Suffering (5:10-11)

"Who called you?" Peter answers his audience,

"the God of all grace" (5:10). A.T. Robertson translates this phrase as "variegated grace," grace in many colors, many forms, many shapes, many styles.[6] "And to what has he called you?" is Peter's second consideration—"to his eternal glory"! Suffering is going to be affecting the lives of these saints, but just for "a little while." The follower of Jesus Christ is to take the long view of the Christian life.

The Pilgrims coped with the worst of times because they envisioned the best of times in the distance. The writer of Hebrews wrote of Jesus suffering in these terms, "Let us fix our eyes on Jesus, the author and perfecter of our faith, who for the joy set before him endured the cross, scorning its shame, and sat down at the right hand of the throne of God" (12:2). In *The Teacher's Commentary* Larry Richards provides this insight:

> Throughout the later letters of our New Testament, hope predominates. We Christians have hope because of our participation in Christ. Even suffering changes when viewed as the the continuation of Jesus' life on earth, and as the life He continues to live through members of the body.[7]

Peter's foreshadowing of the future includes restoration. It adds to the understanding of this promise to realize that the original word for *restore* was used of mending nets.[8] The Great Repairman will sew up the torn and worn nets which were used to fish for souls. This sovereign Lord of history will make the believer strong, firm and stead-fast.

The imperative to stand fast is not a dream, an elusive, unattainable goal; it is very possible and predictable for those who are obedient and Spirit-filled, those who walk in His steps.

Peter brings this section to a climax with a doxology, "To him be the power for ever and ever. Amen" (5:11). The credit is transferred to the God of all grace who has enabled and empowered the suffering saint to successfully survive. The attitude of humility which is worn by the child of God enables the applause and acclamation to be shifted to the One who merits it, the heavenly Father.

Conclusion

God's people must understand that they are involved in spiritual warfare. They must be filled with the Spirit and fully armed. They must go forward in God's strength and not their own. Peter had experienced some losses along the way, but Jesus Christ had restored him (John 21). The deeper life anchors the believer to spiritual resources which are more than sufficient for victory. The first-century believers had some battle scars, but as they placed their confidence in their Commander-in-Chief, Jesus Christ, they would surely and inevitably achieve victory!

The century is different but the equation is still the same:

One + Jesus Christ = Victory!

Discussion Questions for Further Study

1. What are the benefits of humility found in this passage?

2. Is there such an attribute as false humility?

3. How can you resist the devil?

4. To what has God called you?

5. Do you have the "long view" of the Christian life? If not, how can you change?

Endnotes

1. Leon Morris et. al., *Hebrews-Revelation, The Expositor's Bible Commentary*, Vol. 12, ed. Frank E. Gaebelein (Grand Rapids, MI: Zondervan, 1981), 250.

2. C.W. Hall, *Samuel Logan Brengle* (New York: Salvation Army, 1933), 275.

3. A.W. Tozer, *Renewed Day by Day, Vol. 1* (Camp Hill, PA: Christian Publications, 1980), November 9.

4. A.W. Tozer, *I Talk Back to the Devil* (Harrisburg, PA: Christian Publications, 1972), 21.

5. Billy Graham, *Peace with God,* rev. ed. (Waco, TX: Word Books, 1984), 57-58.

6. Archibald Thomas Robertson, *Word Pictures in the New Testament, The General Epistles and the Revelation of John*, Vol. 6 (Grand Rapids, MI: Baker, 1933), 134.

7. Larry Richards, *The Teacher's Commentary* (Wheaton, IL: Victor Books, 1987), 1032.

8. Alan Stibbs, *First Peter, The Tyndale New Testament Commentaries,* rep. ed. (Grand Rapids, MI: Eerdmans, 1983), 174.

11

The Complimentary Close

1 Peter 5:12-14

*With the help of Silas, whom I regard as a
faithful brother, I have written to you briefly,
encouraging you and testifying that this is the
true grace of God. Stand fast in it.*

*She who is in Babylon, chosen together with
you, sends you her greetings, and so does my son
Mark. Greet one another with a kiss of love.*

Peace to all of you who are in Christ.

(1 Peter 5:12-14)

PETER ACKNOWLEDGES THE ASSISTANCE
of Silas in this literary endeavor. Although
we are not sure of his role, whether messenger, manuscript editor or recorder, Silas was instrumental in the effectiveness of this instrument
of instruction for the early Church.

The synergy of friendship is evident throughout the Scriptures. The Old Testament features David and Jonathan as two men that were as close or closer than brothers. Peter's relationship with Mark enabled the latter to write the second Gospel which bears his name. In this greeting Peter designates him as a son. The Pauline writings reveal a number of men to which Paul refers with admiration and affection. Luke, Epaphroditus, Barnabas, Silas and Timothy are friends of the great apostle. The final chapter of Romans includes a recital of friends that are a significant part of Paul's Christian family. It is important to note that several women are commended by Paul, especially Phoebe.

This complimentary close reminds the reader that the Christian life is lived in network with others. The "lone ranger" does not provide a proper model.

First Peter 5:12 is considered by many to be the theme verse of this important document to the men and women who were sanctified by God but scattered as strangers because of their allegiance to Jesus Christ and adherence to His teachings. The apostle evaluates his letter as brief and states its purpose as twofold: *encouragement to its readers* and *testimony to the grace of God* which would enable them to bear clear and consecrated witness in the matrix of the Roman Empire. He returns again to his charge: *"Stand fast!"*

The first-century disciples of Jesus Christ desperately needed encouragement. Peter understood that sometimes a Christian is analogous to the cowardly lion in *The Wizard of Oz*. Brave believers are the expectation, but the faithful can become frozen and timid. At other times a person has done his or her best, but no one affirms the effort or the result.

Now and again there is someone who "puts a lid" on a person who has a great vision or dream for God's glory, convincing this adventurer that they are not capable of achieving a certain goal. And in the despair of sickness, suffering and self-pity, the Christian may need a handkerchief, a hearty prayer, a gesture, a gift. The Church still demands a supply of encouragers.

The word which Peter uses for *encouraging* means to urge forward, like a man pushing another up a hill, or to give advice and counsel, comparable to a therapist helping a person to sort out his or her dilemma, thus activating the will and resolve to go on. The noun form of *encourage* means "one who comes alongside." The word often employed for the Holy Spirit, *paraclete*, means one who *comes alongside to comfort*, counsel and cheerlead the Christian traveler to persevere on the journey. This was the apostle's explicit desire for writing this manuscript: to encourage so that these early adherents of the Christian faith would stand fast!

The first-century Christian was to be tough and resilient through the difficult days of that period of tribulation and dislocation. The steel-like grit and determination that was called for is echoed in a letter by Ignatius to Polycarp, the Bishop of Smyrna who was martyred in his old age. Ignatius' comments are woven with the "stand fast" mind-set. He addresses his bishop with this compelling challenge:

> Just as pilots demand winds and a storm-tossed sailor a harbor, so times like these demand a person like you. . . . Stand your ground like an anvil under the hammer. A great athlete must suffer blows to conquer.[1]

Peter's letter calls for stout and strong Christians in a time of suffering. These men and women could survive because they had internalized the truth of God's Word and had the presence of the Holy Spirit flowing through their existence. It is still an axiom of life that holy people can overcome the liabilities of a hostile society. John wrote, "You, dear children, are from God and have overcome them, because the one who is in you is greater than the one who is in the world" (1 John 4:4).

In First Peter 5:13 Peter identifies his address as Babylon. There are many different opinions as to the meaning of this location, but the most accepted view is that Peter wrote the letter from Rome.

He includes Mark in his final words and calls him a son. Extrabiblical literature links Peter and Mark, and the gospel which Mark wrote is accorded apostolic authority because of this relationship.

Peter advocates the ancient Near Eastern custom of "the kiss of love" or "holy kiss" between believers. This kiss was a common greeting among rabbis as well as a friendly sign of greeting and an emotional token of farewell.[2]

Peter ends his letter as he initiated it with the concept of peace (cf. 1:2). The Hebrews exercised the habit of speaking "shalom," which embraced a holistic peace, the wholeness of man with his world and his God. The Greek word *eirene* is comparable to this blessing in this context.

Peter has left the generations that followed him a treasure. His first letter is a manual in Christian ethics, especially during times of incredible stress and trial. He is commending a lifestyle which is resilient, holiness in the day and the night, in the sunshine and in the shadows. The apostle's objective was to develop, via his letter, a people who were exhibiting internal holiness which could enable them to survive external harassment and hostility.

In his book *The Pure in Heart*, W.E. Sangster wrote: "The best way to approach the study of holiness is not first to seek a definition, but to gaze steadily and long at those in whom, by general consent, this quality appears."[3]

This dynamic church leader, one of the original twelve disciples, endeavored to facilitate character and conduct which corresponded to Jesus Christ. These believers were to follow in His steps. Ralph Waldo Emerson once wrote: "An institution is the lengthened shadow of one person."[4] Christianity was to be the extension of Jesus Christ through men and women. They were to be a replication of Him. They were to "make the invisible Christ visible."

The goal for Peter's readers has remained constant throughout the centuries. The people of God are not to be comfortable in this world; rather they are to be "aliens and strangers," a counterculture, not conformed but transformed. John Stott contends that "the followers of Jesus Christ are to be different—different from both the nominal church and the secular world, different from both the religious and the irreligious."[5]

They are to be a contrast to their culture, and as they embrace the Christian imperatives, the non-negotiables of the faith, they will convert theology into a biography that is destined to have an impact! As Peter's readers then and now embrace the power and truth of this letter they will *be encouraged* and will *stand fast*, riveted to the hope which awaits every pilgrim who pursues the way of Jesus Christ.

Peter dared his audience to aim high. James Russel Lowell penned these thoughts:

> Life is a leaf of paper white
> Whereon each one of us may write
> His word or two, and then come night.
> Greatly begin! though thou have time
> But for a line, be that sublime—
> Not failure, but low aim, is crime.

First Peter is a motivational tool for the Master-life! The centuries have passed since its first circulation, but its message is still contemporary. The elect of God, the redeemed of this world "have been chosen according to the foreknowledge of God the Father, through the sanctifying work of the Spirit, for obedience to Jesus Christ and sprinkling by his blood: Grace and peace be yours in abundance" (1:2).

His letter opens and closes with peace. The life that obeys the Word of God and complies with the commands of God, the imperatives of the Christian faith, will be a faithful and fruitful life, no matter the century, no matter the circumstances.

Discussion Questions for Further Study

1. What Christian friend has most influenced your journey of faith?

2. Who, in your sphere of influence, do you assist in ministry?

3. What are the most difficult situations that confront you as a follower of Jesus Christ?

4. What are ways in which you could encourage someone to "stand fast"?

5. How has your life taken on the aspect of peace in the last twelve months?

Endnotes

[1] Cyril C. Richardson, ed., *Early Christian Fathers* (New York: Macmillan Publishing Company, 1970), 118.

2   Colin Brown, gen. ed., *The New International Dictionary of New Testament Theology*, 3 vols. (Grand Rapids, MI: Zondervan Publishing, 1979), Vol. G-Pre, 549.

3   W.E. Sangster quoted in Marshall Shelley, "From the Editors," *Leadership* (Fall Quarter 1988), 3.

4   Ralph Waldo Emerson, quoted in *Familiar Quotations* by John Barlett, 14th ed., rev., Emily Morison Beck, ed. (Boston: Little, Brown & Co., 1968), 606.

5   John R.W. Stott, *Christian Counter-Culture* (Downers Grove, IL: Intervarsity Press, 1978), 19.

12

A Summary of First Peter's Crucial Content

PETER LABELED HIS LETTER BRIEF (5:12) but compared to most letters written by today's readers it is rather lengthy (105 verses). His purpose was to encourage these scattered believers to stand fast in their faith during a demanding era of Christian history. He challenged them to tie a knot and hold on! The first century provided a major test for these new disciples who embraced the Person and message of Jesus! And the apostle reached deep into his own soul to coauthor with the Holy Spirit a prescription to enable these "strangers and aliens" not only to survive but to shine for their Lord and God.

Peter refers to *suffering* a minimum of *one dozen times*. He did not duck the issue but dealt with it head-on. He spoke of the value of suffering and compared it to a *refiner's fire* which would produce a product worth more than gold. He linked suffering Christians to the suffering Christ and ordered them to follow in His steps. Peter looked at the believer's cross and saw it as a plus sign, an opportunity to vindicate and substantiate the deeper life which was being experienced by these early adherents of Christianity.

The Spirit also led Peter to project the long view of their suffering which prompted them to look up and beyond their present trials to a much brighter day of triumph and reward. He cast the vision of the end of their journey, not just the pain of their present moment. He painted a living hope in a living Christ. This was the antidote that he dispensed to a much maligned and much oppressed early band of believers.

The subtitle of this commentary, *Strategic Imperatives for Suffering Saints,* narrows the latitude and restricts the options of not only Peter's readers, but also the contemporary audience. There are nonnegotiables, core values, which must be obeyed if the follower of Jesus Christ is to win the spiritual war.

The author of this letter projected the theme of *submission* at various junctures within the letter. To submit is to follow the commands of another, to comply with the commands of one above you. The actual original Greek word which Peter used for *submit, hupotasso,* is a military term which amplifies the imperative nature of the directives which are given. Peter demands submission in the context of marriage, in respect to civil authorities and even for leaders (shepherds) of the Church who are accountable to a Chief Shepherd.

In an age of assertiveness these calls to submit may seem like ancient ethics which are anachronistic and obsolete. But submission is part and parcel of Christ's own biography as He willingly submitted to the Father's will.

A third theme that is sprinkled throughout the letter involves the attitude of *service*. The fisherman casts this line into the waters of his manuscript several times. Not only did he summon these believers to serve God, but he focused that general theme by commending them to serve each other with harmony and hospitality. Peter was explicit that they should even serve non-Christians, pagans, and by so doing become servants of Jesus Christ.

He made a sweeping plea for service when he wrote in 2:17, "Show proper respect to everyone: Love the brotherhood of believers, fear God, honor the king." The all-inclusiveness of such a directive must be met by a servant's heart, especially when the "king" may have been Nero, who chose to blame the Christians and to punish them for the fire which engulfed Rome.

Suffering, submission and service are only paper tigers if a fourth theme is not a reality in the life of the believer. *Sanctification*, the process of holiness, is a cornerstone of Peter's letter. He incorporated a brief treatise on this issue early in the letter. Drawing upon the Old Testament, he recycled the command, "Be holy, because I am holy" (Leviticus 11:44, etc.).

Holiness was the expectation for these pioneers of the Christian faith. The fullness of Jesus Christ within their hearts would permit these men and women to "make the invisible Christ visible" and enable them to convert what they knew about God and Jesus Christ to biography. Without the presence of the Holy Spirit, these men and women were doomed to be frustrated failures. With the Spirit indwelling them they were "a chosen people, a royal priesthood, a holy nation" (2:9).

Significance for Today's Reader

Is this letter relevant for today's disciple or is its value confined to Christians scattered throughout the Roman provinces almost two millennia ago?

First Peter speaks today because it wrestles with issues that are still divisive in the contemporary believer's life experience. This ancient letter calls Christians to be a counterculture. The reality of the American culture in the late twentieth century is that the term *post-Christian* can be applied without much debate. The redeemed are bombarded with the siren songs of an existential, humanistic age which acts as if situation ethics is sacred. The higher Christian life is not a prevailing norm. The label "stranger" and "alien" should still be legitimate as it was in the first century.

First Peter provides some compass-accurate directions which outline the expectations for the Christian life. This brief book provides a mission statement for living as a light in a dark world. There is a desperate need for Christians to function as priests who present the needs of men and women to God, who present God's Word and will to that same audience and who model Jesus Christ in their day seasons and night seasons.

Peter's vision to look beyond this world is so strategic for those who live in affluent nations and comfortable times. Believers face the temptation of some of the Egyptians who, during the empire's zenith, hoped that the next world would only be as good as this world. God's people need to remember that we are not citizens of this world but that "our citizenship is in heaven. And we eagerly await a Savior from there, the Lord Jesus Christ" (Philippians 3:20).

Finally, there is suffering which comes in diverse and sundry forms. As I compose this concluding chapter I am freshly aware of deep and painful circumstances which have affixed themselves to the members and friends (the flock) of the church I help shepherd. There are believers who are still misunderstood by their families, there are "mixed faith" marriages, there are struggles to submit to a multitude of authorities, including church, civil, marital, parental, educational. Submission is still a tough ticket to sell, especially when the focus of authority rests with an unbeliever. Christians still face the problem of pain and the challenge of perseverance. This letter is still good medicine.

The Deeper Life

"If you are insulted because of the name of

Christ, you are blessed, for the Spirit of glory and
of God rests on you" (1 Peter 4:14).

Peter prescribed a big pill to swallow in that
verse. To be insulted and say, "I'm blessed," is
only possible through the Spirit of God resting on
you. To be able to resonate Jesus Christ in times
of distress, to bend and not break, to view suffering as a tool in the hands of a sovereign God—
these challenges demand the deeper life.

The surrender to God of one's whole inventory
of life, gifts, financial resources, family, health and
most importantly, the key to one's heart, opens up
a whole new possibility—Christ in me (see Colossians 1:27).

This is the deeper life—to entrust everything,
even one's suffering, to the heavenly Father and
His Son, Jesus Christ.

The imperatives of the Christian life become
just suggestions without the presence and power
of the Holy Spirit. Peter has presented a most
compelling rationale for standing fast, but without
the energy and purity of the Holy Spirit, the student will fail the exam. It is the wellsprings of the
Spirit which see us through the dry and dusty
times.

I would like to conclude this commentary with
a prayer made by John Huss just two weeks prior
to his death, which was ordered because he had
strongly advocated the truth of God's Word. As
he stood on the threshold of death and prepared to
face eternity he prayed:

O Most Holy Christ . . . give me a fearless heart, a right faith, a firm hope, a perfect love, that for thy sake I may lay down my life with patience and joy. Amen![1]

I believe Peter would have added his own "amen" to that prayer.

May those who study First Peter emerge with a fearless heart, an orthodox faith, a bedrock hope, a more perfect love, and may they face the opponents of the Christian faith with patience and joy.

Discussion Questions for Further Study

1. What verse or verses in First Peter stand(s) out to you as the most beneficial or applicable to your own experience?

2. What role does the deeper life play in fulfilling the imperatives Peter emphasizes in this letter?

3. What imperative do you find most difficult to carry out?

4. In what context could you recommend to a friend or family member reading and applying this book?

5. If you were writing a hymn or chorus on First Peter, what would you give as a title?

Endnote

[1] E.H. Broadbent, *The Pilgrim Church* (London: Pickering and Inglis, 1955), 124-125.

SELECTED BIBLIOGRAPHY

I: Works on First Peter

Barclay, William, *The Letters of James and Peter, The Daily Study Bible Series*, Vol. 14 (Philadelphia: Westminster Press), 1976.

Fickett, Harold L., Jr., *Peter's Principles* (Ventura, CA: Regal Books, 1974).

Hebrews-Revelation, The Expositor's Bible Commentary, 12 vols .Gaebelein, Frank E., gen. ed. (Grand Rapids, MI: Zondervan, 1981), Vol. 14.

Robertson, Archibald Thomas, *Word Pictures in the New Testament, The General Epistles and the Revelation of John, 6 vols. (Grand Rapids, MI: Baker, 1933), Vol. 6.*

Stibbs, Alan M., and Walls, Andrew F., *First Peter. The Tyndale New Testament Commentaries*, reprint edition (Grand Rapids, MI: Eerdmans, 1983).

Simpson, A.B., *The Epistles of Peter, John and Jude* (Harrisburg, PA: Christian Publications, n.d.)

Wiersbe, Warren, *Be Hopeful* (Wheaton, IL: Scripture Press, 1982).

II: General Works

Augsburger, David, *The Freedom of Forgiveness* (Chicago: MoodyPress, 1970).

Barker, Kenneth, ed., *The NIV Study Bible* (Grand Rapids, MI: Zondervan, 1985).

Barna, George, *The Power of Vision* (Ventura, CA: Regal Books, 1992).

Bellah, Robert, et. al., Habits of the Heart (Berkeley, CA: University of California Press, 1985).

Bridges, Jerry, *The Pursuit of Holiness* (Colorado Springs, CO: NavPress, 1978).

Browning, Robert, "Rabbi Ben Ezra," 1864.

Chafer, Lewis Perry, and Walvoord, John F., *Major Bible Themes,* rev. ed. (Grand Rapids, MI: Zondervan, 1974).

Chambers, Oswald., *Daily Thoughts for Disciples* (Grand Rapids, MI: Zondervan, 1990).

Clark, Mary, trans. *Book Nine: Confessions, Augustine of Hippo: Selected Writings* (New York: Paulist Press, 1984).

Covey, Stephen, *Seven Habits of Highly Effective People* (New York: Simon and Schuster, 1989).

Elliott, Elisabeth, *Let Me Be a Woman* (Wheaton, IL: Tyndale, 1988).

Eusebius, *History of the Church,* IV.

Finney, Charles G., *Crystal Christianity* (Pittsburgh, PA: Whitaker House, 1985).

Foster, Richard, *Celebration of Discipline*, rev. ed. (San Francisco: Harper, 1988).

Graham, Billy, *Peace with God*, rev. ed. (Waco, TX: Word Books, 1984).

_____, *World Aflame* (Minneapolis, MN: Billy Graham Evangelistic Association, 1965).

Harrison, Everett F., *Introduction to the New Testament* (Grand Rapids, MI: Eerdmans, 1964).

Henry, Matthew, *Commentary on the Whole Bible* (Grand Rapids, MI: Zondervan, 1980).

Jones, E. Stanley, *Abundant Living* (Nashville, TN: Abingdon Press, 1942).

Luther, Martin, *Works of Martin Luther*, 6 vols. (Grand Rapids, MI: Baker, 1982), Vol. 2.

Mains, David, *The Dysfunctional Church* (Wheaton, IL: Victor Books, 1992).

Maxwell, John, *The Winning Attitude* (San Bernadino, CA: Here's Life Publishers, 1992).

Men's Devotional Bible (Grand Rapids, MI: Zondervan, 1993).

Nietzche, Friedrich, *Beyond Good and Evil*, trans. Helen Zimmern (London: 1907).

Packer, J.I., *Knowing God* (Downers Grove, IL: InterVarsity Press, 1973).

Peterson, Eugene, *A Long Obedience in the Same Direction* (Downers Grove, IL: InterVarsity Press, 1980).

Richards, Larry, *The Teacher's Commentary* (Wheaton, IL: Victor Books, 1987).

Richardson, Cyril, ed., *Early Christian Fathers* (New York: Macmillan, 1970).

Sanders, J. Oswald, *In Pursuit of Maturity* (Grand Rapids, MI: Zondervan, 1986).

_____, *Spiritual Leadership* (Chicago: Moody Press, 1994).

Schlossberg, Herbert, *Idols for Destruction* (Nashville, TN: Thomas Nelson, 1983).

Simpson, A.B., *Days of Heaven on Earth* (Camp Hill, PA: Christian Publications, 1984).

_____, *Gifts and Graces* (Camp Hill, PA: Christian Publications, 1993).

_____, *Missionary Messages* (Camp Hill, PA: Christian Publications, 1987).

Stott, John, *One People* (Old Tappan, NJ: Revell, 1968).

Stowell, Joseph M., *Shepherding the Church into the 21st Century* (Wheaton, IL: Victor Books, 1994).

Swindoll, Charles, *The Quest for Character* (Portland, OR: Multnomah Press, 1987).

_____, *Strike the Original Match* (Portland, OR: Multnomah Press, 1980).

Ten Boom, Corrie, *The Hiding Place* (Washington Depot, CT: Chosen Books, 1971).

Torrance, David W., and Torrance, Thomas F., eds., *The Epistles of Paul the Apostle to the Galatians, Ephesians, Philippians and Colossians, Calvin's Commentaries*, trans. T.H.L. Parker, Vol. 3 (Grand Rapids, MI: Eerdmans, 1974).

Tozer, A.W., *How to Be Filled with the Holy Spirit* (Camp Hill, PA: Christian Publications, n.d.).

_____, *I Talk Back to the Devil* (Harrisburg, PA: Christian Publications, 1972).

_____, *Renewed Day by Day, Vol. 1*, (Camp Hill, PA: Christian Publications, 1980).

_____, *The Knowledge of the Holy*. (San Francisco: Harper and Row, 1961).

Unger, Merrill F., *Unger's Bible Dictionary* (Chicago: Moody Press, 1966), 3rd ed.

Vincent, M.R., *Word Studies in the New Testament*, 2 vols. (MacDill AFB, FL: MacDonald Publishing, 1986).

Vine, W.E., *Expository Dictionary of New Testament Words*, 4 vols. (Grand Rapids, MI: Zondervan, 1952), Vol. 3, Lo-Ser.

Wagner, C. Peter, Your Spiritual Gifts Can Help Your Church Grow (Ventura, CA: Regal Books, 1979).

Wilkinson, Bruce H., exec. ed., *Closer Walk Bible* (Grand Rapids, MI: Zondervan, 1992).

_____, exec. ed., *Closer Walk New Testament* (Grand Rapids, MI: Zondervan, 1990).

Wright, Christopher, J.H., *An Eye for an Eye* (Downers Grove, IL: InterVarsity Press, 1983).

Yancey, Philip, *Where Is God When It Hurts?* (Grand Rapids, MI: Zondervan, 1977).

RECOMMENDED READING

I found the following sources to be particularly significant in the writing of this commentary:

William Barclay's *Daily Study Bible* provided some illuminating notes on the history and background of the first century. Barclay's metaphors are often classic.

The New International Dictionary of New Testament Theology, with Colin Brown serving as general editor, provides insightful scholarship on Greek words without drowning the user in trivia.

The Expositor's Bible Commentary was crisp and practical in its consideration of Peter's small but significant letter. I find it to be one of the most readable of the modern commentary sets.

Archibald Thomas Robertson's *Word Pictures in the New Testament* continues to provide key data on New Testament words. Sometimes his vernacular is outdated but the positive contributions far outweigh the liabilities of aging terminology.

The Tyndale New Testament Commentary on First
Peter written primarily by Alan Stibbs, provided
some fresh research and articulate explanations.
I am indebted to R. Kent Hughes' commentary on
Ephesians for many of the format ideas. His new
Preaching the Word series combines sound scholar-
ship, clear writing and practical applications.